Arvo Pärt

OUT OF SILENCE

Arvo Pärt

Out of Silence

PETER C. BOUTENEFF

ST VLADIMIR'S SEMINARY PRESS
YONKERS, NEW YORK
2015

Library of Congress Cataloging-in-Publication Data

Bouteneff, Peter
     Arvo Pärt : out of silence / Peter C. Bouteneff
         pages   cm
     Includes bibliographical references
     ISBN 978-0-88141-512-4 (pbk.) — ISBN 978-0-88141-513-1 (electronic)
     1. Pärt, Arvo—Criticism and interpretation.   2. Music—Religious aspects—
Christianity.   I. Title.

ML410.P1755B68 2015
780.92—dc23

                                                                    2015006956

Special thanks to Carnegie Hall &
The Metropolitan Museum of Art
for permission to reproduce concert photographs,
and to Elizabeth Bouteneff for rendering the Alina *flower.*

© 2015 BY PETER C. BOUTENEFF

ST VLADIMIR'S SEMINARY PRESS
575 Scarsdale Road, Yonkers, NY 10707
1–800–204–2665
www.svspress.com

ISBN 978-0-88141-512-4

PRINTED IN THE UNITED STATES OF AMERICA

The publication of this book is made possible by a generous gift from Bob and Connie Abodeely.

de profundis clamavi ad te Domine
Psalm 130:1

Ἐν ἀρχῇ ἦν ὁ λόγος, καὶ ὁ λόγος ἦν πρὸς τὸν θεόν,
καὶ θεὸς ἦν ὁ λόγος.

John 1:1

I had to draw this music gently
out of silence and emptiness.

Arvo Pärt

Contents

INTRODUCTION

This is a book about Arvo Pärt's music, explored in terms of his faith and life. Given that listeners so often speak of the impact of his music in terms of spirituality, and given Pärt's own spiritual home in the Orthodox Church, it felt appropriate to draw some lines of correlation between his music and the theology and experience of that Eastern Christian faith. One goal of this book, then, is to bring listeners to a fuller appreciation of what is going on in the composer's work.

Conversations about this remarkable music, especially by its more avid listeners, often feature a "my first encounter with Arvo Pärt" story. On our way toward an immersion into that world, I thought I would give you mine so that you might know whose company you are keeping as you read this book.

I actually met the man before encountering his music. It was during the early 1990s: Pärt and I found ourselves visiting the same monastery for a week, where a mutual friend made sure to introduce us. Pärt was, after all, a famous composer, and I had earned degrees in both music and theology. But as it was, I had never knowingly heard a note of his music. I had not actually even heard of him. We spent hours walking together and talking on themes of mutual interest, among them the phenomenon of "Holy Foolishness" on which I had just written a thesis. At one point I asked him about his music, what it was like, what kinds of instrumentation he employed. He chatted about it with no pretense or fanfare: "Sometimes I write for choir, sometimes for orchestra. Or the organ . . ." I had the sense that if he was famous—and it turned out that by this time, he really was—he was probably enjoying the opportunity to talk to someone who was neither an awe-struck admirer nor a jaded music critic. I enjoyed his company immensely, but what did his music sound like? What were the chances that I would even like it?

Within a matter of weeks, upon my return to Oxford where I was studying toward my doctorate, I noticed that Pärt's *Passio* was being performed in the New College Chapel, so I bought a ticket. Readers familiar with this composition—a searingly intense and dramatic 70-minute work with a breathtaking conclusion—can only imagine how it served to introduce Pärt to a first-time lis-tener. I will return to discuss the piece at this book's conclusion, but for the moment I will say that my experience of that concert began a new relationship with music, a heightened understanding of the possibilities of art.

I wondered: What would it be like, now, to meet Pärt again (as I would some weeks later)? Inevitably it was more difficult to have a conversation as if among peers: I had been transformed into one of his rapt fans. Happily, that didn't prevent us from having several memorable encounters. One evening I went to his house with two monks and a fellow layman from Russia, and we sang for Arvo and his wife Nora a Georgian church hymn. After dinner Arvo got out his portable CD player and played for us the just-released *Miserere*, carefully adjusting the volume throughout, compensat-ing for that composition's broad dynamic range. He remained the person I had already come to know: a completely unpretentious and unassuming person, who talked about things that mattered but also knew how to joke and laugh. And who took music utterly seriously, as he did the Church's liturgical and prayer life.

This Book: For Whom, and Why?

In seeking to deepen people's experience of Pärt's music, another goal of this study is to reach as much as possible his broadly diverse audience. His listeners—religious believers, agnostics, atheists, the "spiritual but not religious"—all draw from the same well, even if they bring different vessels to it. However, not all of his audience is convinced of the need for a discussion of the spiritual foundations of the man and his music. That need is obvious to some, not to all. The Arvo Pärt Centre currently being established in Estonia reports frequent inquiries on this subject. Commentaries on Pärt never fail to mention the composer's affiliation with the Orthodox Church, but rarely go into detail about it. They are either at a loss for more to say or convinced that there *is* no more to say. Yet when his music is so frequently called "spiritual," either because of or in spite of the predominantly sacred texts that underlie it, are there really no connections to be explored, even if tentatively, propositionally?

Forays in this direction already exist. Some have begun to analyze the spirituality of Pärt's œuvre from a secular perspective—a confessional *tabula rasa*, as it were.[1] Others have begun to excavate the Orthodox tradition and found some promising leads in hesychasm and in the apophatic tradition.[2] I have been encouraged

---

[1]For example, Robert Sholl, "Arvo Pärt and Spirituality," in *The Cambridge Companion to Arvo Pärt,* ed. Andrew Shenton (Cambridge: Cambridge University Press, 2012).

[2]Cf. Paul Hillier, *Arvo Pärt*, Oxford Studies of Composers (Oxford: Oxford University Press, 1997), 1–23.

by a number of Pärt's listeners, scholars, and critics who have awaited a study on him from an Orthodox Christian perspective. I realize, however, that others are entirely unconvinced that such a study is necessary at all.

One music writer noted recently, "Arvo Pärt's music has such universal appeal that it is easy to lose sight of the specific spiritual traditions that feed it."[3] She has identified the paradox: universal appeal, particular tradition. But once again, is it useful to poke around the composer's particular spiritual background? I would begin the response with a focus on the role of "particularity" in regard to spiritual traditions. And the fact here is that no theology, no spirituality, exists disembodied from particular contexts. Many themes are omnipresent in the great spiritual traditions (e.g., the pursuit of unity and integration, the overcoming of evil and suffering), but each is expressed by distinct people in distinct settings, almost always as part of existing communities with customs, schools of thought, and practices. Each, then, makes its own mark on these universal questions. On the matter of suffering, for example, Christianity and Buddhism will say different, if periodically overlapping things. And within the Christian traditions of the East and West you will find different emphases and insights as well. The particular, then, is an inevitability.

On that basis I would argue that when a cultural figure professes adherence to a specific faith tradition, and produces art that speaks to some of its central themes, we are rightly interested in what that tradition actually asserts. Consider some examples:

---

[3]Corinna da Fonseca-Wollheim, "'Adam's Lament' and Other Choral Works," in *The New York Times*, October 28, 2012 (print).

The appeal of the current Dalai Lama is broad. He exudes simultaneously compassion, playfulness, and seriousness. His teachings bespeak wisdom with a practical applicability that reaches vast audiences of all backgrounds. Yet if someone wanted to come closer to his teaching, his word, his way, at some point she would need to grapple with Tibetan Buddhism. The Dalai Lama is through and through a Tibetan Buddhist—indeed he is the principal personal representation of that faith.

The Russian novelist Fyodor Dostoyevsky might serve as a more pertinent example since, although an Orthodox Christian, he does not fulfill the same iconic function. Broadly speaking, readers receive *The Brothers Karamazov* as a riveting piece of literature. But a reader's understanding of the conversation between Ivan and Alyosha, of the Grand Inquisitor parable, and of the episodes involving Staretz Zosima, are indisputably enriched by understanding Orthodox Christian tradition, teaching, and monasticism, not to mention Orthodox relations with Roman Catholicism. These constitute Dostoevsky's spiritual and intellectual roots; these are what give rise to his narratives and his *dramatis personae.*

Not all artists bring a particular faith to bear on their work, but when they do, however diverse their results, studying these connections makes sense. A serious student of the American composer and music theorist John Cage will eventually be forced to reckon with his relationship to Buddhism and the *I Ching*, which influenced his aleatoric method. One who seeks to penetrate the French composer and organist Olivier Messiaen cannot get around his Roman Catholicism. Bereft of encounters with the belief system and tradition that so influenced their output, their audiences may enjoy their artistry well enough, but not fathom them as closely as they might.

So it is with Pärt. "To really understand his music," Nora Pärt has been quoted saying about her husband's work, "you must first understand how this religious tradition [Orthodox Christianity] flows through him." To which Arvo adds, "If anybody wishes to understand me, they must listen to my music; if anybody wishes to know my 'philosophy', then they can read any of the Church Fathers."[4]

Thus the critical principle underlying this book: insights from the Orthodox Christian spiritual tradition are capable of shedding important light on Arvo Pärt's musical output. There is, however, neither the need nor the possibility of establishing actual *causality*. We are not here to establish that the Orthodox Church's theology has directly inspired or given rise to Pärt's compositional style, his impulse to compose in particular tonalities, or his understanding of suffering and hope. But the possibilities of *correlation* are compelling.

Methodology

Connecting Pärt's art and his faith carries potential dangers that I will seek at all costs to avoid. In that spirit, I will never say nor imply that the music is only for the believer, or that Pärt composes especially for religious believers. He himself emphasizes that his

---

[4]Lewis Owens, "Arvo Pärt : Miserere : Miserere And Minimalism," *Spike Magazine,* June 1, 2000. Online at http://www.spikemagazine.com/0600arvopart.php, accessed November 5, 2012. Nora is ever increasingly a part of Arvo Pärt's published interviews. The composer himself often turns to her to help express aspects of his music.

work is for everyone and anyone. I will likewise not claim that Orthodox Christian theology holds the hidden key to Pärt's music, without which it cannot be appreciated. I will, however, suggest that insights from Orthodox tradition, liturgy, and theology carry relevance and affect a listener's experience of the music. His faith and the sacred texts on which much of his music is based are all right there in front of us. It would be disingenuous to underplay these factors.

Two more things I am not doing: I am not writing this in order to preach Orthodox Christian theology, although I will be explaining those aspects that are relevant to Pärt's work. And I am not setting out to be comprehensive or definitive. This book, consisting in propositions and reflections, aims to elicit further work. As far as my approach vis-à-vis musicology and theology, let me say something about each.

Specialization and Terminology

Although its subject is ultimately music—specifically, music composed according to particular principles and rules—this is not primarily a musicological study. Such essays on Pärt's work are happily proliferating. The present book will periodically enter the realms of theory, history, and music criticism as demanded by the subject matter, but my analyses will not be technical enough to depend on extensive musical training. The intention is that they be just deep enough to satisfy the purposes of the book, alienating neither the untrained ear nor the music professional.

As for spirituality and theology, it will be more challenging to hit all the right notes, as it were. A few readers of this book may be experienced theologians who find the treatment here to be lightweight; my hope is that the way I have configured these materials, in relation to Pärt's life and work, will still be useful. But the book is intended at least as much for people of different faiths or none in particular, as well as people who are disenchanted by the enterprise of organized religion. To such readers, I should say up front that this book will periodically get theological, maybe more (and specifically more *Christian*) than you will feel comfortable with. I ask your indulgence and hope you find it repaid. The book will also reflect my own training and lived experience in both music and in the theology, liturgy, and faith of the Orthodox Church. I am working on the principle that a deep and personal engagement in the things that are studied will serve, rather than impede, my analysis.

Critical Detachment

On that score, a common presupposition in scholarship is that the most useful study of a subject is the one coming from a place of detachment, the idea being that a mind stripped of all prejudices and presumption will be best positioned to reach neutral conclusions. This ideal, within both sciences and humanities, has lately been dismantled by showing that some of the best research and insightful observations come from those who are deeply and personally involved in their subject, precisely by virtue of that engagement.[5] As you have seen, I am deeply engaged with the subject, both musically and theologically. In this book we are not looking for neutral conclusions; we are looking for involvement.

---

[5]Andrew Louth, *Discerning the Mystery: An Essay on the Nature of Theology* (Oxford: Oxford University Press, 1983) is especially helpful. See esp. "Dissociation of Sensibility," in ibid., 1–16.

Authorial intent

Mid-twentieth-century literary theory has it that an author's process, life, and certainly his or her intent, properly has no bearing or authority on the understanding of the art. Currents building on the New Criticism place the entire onus of interpretation on the audience.[6] Either way, the art no longer belongs to the artist, whose life, context, and motivations are held to be both inscrutable and irrelevant. Even if one might temper this extreme disregard for the person of the author, we must acknowledge a certain disconnect between author and audience. If the disconnect is obvious, its repercussions are not. As regards this matter, my approach is similar to Pärt's own: to give a sense of what that is, I will let Pärt weigh in:

> As often with art, you have the problem of the disconnect between the creator/the creative process, and the observer/listener. But is the disconnect complete? Moments of recognition between composer and listener happen somehow, like sitting in two passing trains. You only make out the person in the other train during a fleeting glance through the window. We composers have our path to follow, and the listeners theirs. [. . .] And still, we meet: through music, let's say.[7]

"And still we meet." Pärt does not believe that the disconnect is complete, neither do I, and chances are that neither do you,

---

[6] A recent summary of the question, whose conclusions I agree with, may be found in Robert C. Saler, *Between Magisterium and Marketplace: A Constructive Account of Theology and the Church*, Emerging Scholars (Minneapolis, MN: Fortress, 2014), 23–49.

[7] Geoff Smith, "Sources of Invention: An Interview with Arvo Pärt," *The Musical Times* 140, no. 1868 (Autumn 1999).

otherwise you would not be reading a book that seeks to give insight into the music precisely by exploring the composer's spiritual universe. It follows that I will at points be drawing directly on the composer's experience, sometimes in his own words, and in those of his wife Nora, herself a trained musician with important insights into his work. They will not be invoked as the final authority, but as voices eminently worth listening to.

Sources

Engagement will entail subjective opinions, listeners' personal impressions, sometimes including my own. Here too I would re-emphasize Pärt's singular ability to speak spiritually to a diverse audience. I have likewise been interested in reaching and hearing from a wide range of listeners, and so will be drawing on the existing scholarly literature, CD liner notes, music criticism, as well as from comments found on social media.

Background and Acknowledgments

This book grew out of my longstanding relationship with Pärt's music. As mentioned earlier, that relationship has its foundations in an association with the composer himself begun in 1990. In December 2011, St Vladimir's Seminary, where I teach, approached Arvo and Nora Pärt with a three-fold proposal: to honor the composer academically with a doctoral degree, and to celebrate him musically with concerts of the highest caliber in the New York area. We discussed also an ongoing project that would begin to explore the connection between his music and the Orthodox tradition that he considers his spiritual home. Thus was born the Arvo Pärt Project that has so far resulted in memorable and critically acclaimed concerts at Carnegie Hall and the Metropolitan Museum of Art in New York,[8] the John F. Kennedy Center and the Phillips Collection in Washington, DC (the composer's first appearance on the US East Coast since 1984), courses, lectures, and cross-disciplinary panel discussions, and this book. It has been a remarkable journey. Throughout, Arvo and Nora Pärt have generously shared stories and insights with me that have proved indispensable to this study.

The Arvo Pärt Project is lodged at St Vladimir's Seminary, whose dean and chancellor, staff, and trustees have courageously supported its work. My co-director in the Project, Nicholas Reeves, has been a constant source of wisdom, musical advice, and creative friendship. The staff of the Arvo Pärt Centre in Laulasmaa, Estonia, were of great help as the book's manuscript took shape—with special thanks to Kristina Kõrver. Alexander Lingas made many insightful comments on the draft, especially as regards the relationship of music and text, and helped steer me away from significant errors. Robert Saler reviewed the text and provided many useful comments, and Patricia Fann Bouteneff, as editor, played a crucial role in shaping my prose. I have benefited greatly from exchanging ideas with many avid Pärt listeners and authorities, notably Alex Ambrose, Laurie Anderson, Jeffers Engelhardt, James Jordan, Alan Teder and Limor Tomer. Paul Hillier, whose monograph on Pärt remains unsurpassed and whose association with the composer has made an indelible mark on the sound of

---

[8]May 31, 2014 at Carnegie Hall, Isaac Stern Auditorium (sold out), with the Tallinn Chamber Orchestra and the Estonian Philharmonic Chamber Choir, conducted by Tõnu Kaljuste. June 2, 2014, at the Temple of Dendur, Sackler Wing of the Metropolitan Museum of Art (sold out), with the Estonian Philharmonic Chamber Choir, conducted by Tõnu Kaljuste.

his music, shared important insights with me early on in this study and gave me generous encouragement. I have been fortunate to draw on the ever-growing body of texts by scholars and critics who know and love Pärt's music and have articulated profound insights about it; I refer to many of them throughout the book. May their number continue to increase so that the conversation might expand, and so that this remarkable music continues to get the listening it deserves.

The organization of this book

In this study we will visit three broad spaces. In Part I my aim is to set out first principles. Having addressed above why a study of Pärt vis-à-vis Orthodox Christianity might be useful and for whom, I will take that question further into an examination of what is meant by "spirituality" and "religion," as these subjects are ever-present in reactions to Pärt's work. Discussing the "Arvo Pärt Phenomenon"—how Pärt's music often reaches its listeners' spiritual selves—will be a way of insuring that this book be guided at least as much by those listeners as by my own preoccupations and predilections. I will also discuss what people have begun to say about Pärt's Orthodox Christian affiliation, look at the compositions that reflect that affiliation explicitly, and recount something of how the composer came to find, and join, the Orthodox Church.

This section will conclude with a more protracted study of the role of text in people's experience of Pärt's work, and in the composer's own writing process. Most of Pärt's work is texted; with very few exceptions the texts are sacred. The repercussions of that fact are significant, if sometimes surprising.

Part II will explore the theme of silence. This will entail looking into Pärt's own "silent" years during which he composed little. We will be looking at musical, political, and spiritual factors that informed what came before and during that important transitional period. Silence is often identified as being a quality inherent in Pärt's music; the music intentionally incorporates it. This section will also feature an extended reflection on the nature of silence and stillness in Orthodox Christian tradition: their different characteristics and their role in the process of creativity and in the cultivation of inner quietude and prayer.

The third space we will be visiting concerns dualities held in unity. Pärt's music is typically said to marry antinomies of sensibility: lament and hope, sorrow and consolation, straying and stability. The composer himself invokes other metaphors that carry explicitly theological implications: sin and forgiveness, the human and the divine. I will be endeavoring to trace this theme—the yoking of dualities—running through the biblical, ascetical, and theological tradition, right up to its profound expression in the writings and life of the twentieth-century Orthodox *staretz* St Silouan—to whom Pärt is so spiritually drawn. The twin voices that constitute the *tintinnabuli* compositional style bear a clear relationship to the affective realities being conveyed. This musical analysis will gain a deeper meaning through correlation with theological principles.

I: Points of Entry

Spirituality and Religion

I have been saying that listeners often speak of their experience of Arvo Pärt's music in terms of "spirituality," which immediately brings the question of what that actually means. The use of this word in our day has become problematic because it is both so broad as to be useless and so common as to be nearly inevitable. It is virtually meaningless if it comes to stand for too much. Yet it is inevitable, in so far as we need a word that speaks to our intimations of the transcendent. We need a word that is *im*precise enough to do justice both to the inherent mystery of its subject—the spirit is not something that can be pinned down, observed, and decisively defined—and to the evident diversity of practices and traditions, religious and secular, that invoke or perceive it. And yet when such a word comes to speak of all that is mystical across all traditions and no particular tradition, defined and undefined alike, it becomes diffuse to the point of being useless. Yet, because religion holds no monopoly on experiences of the ineffable, we return to the need for a word that speaks to the things that take people beyond themselves, intimations of realities that go beyond the perceived causal nexus.

Although there are definitions of spirituality that people seem to hold in common, centering on transcendence, the particular concepts and experiences of it are diverse. This means that "the spirituality of Arvo Pärt's music" is going to mean different things to different listeners, in large part dictated by their experience, big or small, with the mystical or "numinous," with God, with nature, with prayer—and with religion.

"Spiritual" and "religious" are potentially overlapping qualifiers. Some people, whatever their views on religion, speak of "religious experience" as synonymous with "spiritual experience."[1] Yet others experience spirituality and religion as things that are distinct or even opposed. The category of "spiritual but not religious," so popular as to have become cliché, testifies to the relatively recent perception of a clear split between the two.[2] Before discussing "spirituality" and explaining how I will use that word in this study, we need to look at the word "religion."

Religion

In a neutral, historical definition, religions are systems of faith and worship. (The fact of being systematized makes the expression "organized religion" a redundancy.) But the point of their organization is less important than their inherently *communal* nature. One who is religious is effectively marrying his or her personal faith and worship with that of an existing *body* of faithful, a group that has a structure, a history, a tradition. As such, religions are communities existing in the present but extending to

[1]See, e.g., Ann Taves, *Religious Experience Reconsidered: A Building-Block Approach to the Study of Religion and Other Special Things* (Princeton, NJ: Princeton University Press, 2009).

[2]On this split, see especially Charles Taylor, *A Secular Age* (Cambridge, MA: Belknap/Harvard University Press, 2007), 505–535. It is a searching and not unsympathetic account of the road to the present situation.

the past. To the degree that religions find expression in texts, art, music, philosophy and theology, and political structures they are inherently also cultural phenomena.

In so far as religion deals with transcendent, often non-material realities, its core content is "spiritual." And yet, precisely because religion is so enmeshed with culture and politics, often in profoundly ambiguous ways, and because it appears to tether the flights of the inner self, "religion" can carry negative associations as well, not only for avowed atheists but for people with an abiding faith in the spiritual. Even "religious" people can harbor decisively pejorative definitions of religion. For Swiss Reformed theologian Karl Barth, as well as for Orthodox theologian Alexander Schmemann, "religion" is the antithesis of genuine Christianity; it is akin to superstition. They see religion as humanity's self-justification before a god that it created in its own image.[3] Authentic Christianity, to such thinkers, is not a religion: it is genuine life, fully oriented in Jesus Christ.

Even as we bear in mind the kinds of connotations that "religion" can summon, this study will be best served by a neutral and historical/cultural definition. Along those lines, as ethereal as its spiritual subject may be, religion—as a historical, communal, cultural phenomenon—works through tangible things, words, and actions: through prayer, ritual, text, meditation. Religion has historically resulted in particular texts, rites, practices, theology, all of which pertain to spiritual realities. In this vein and for our purposes, we would note that the texts Arvo Pärt sets to music are,

---

[3]See Karl Barth, *On Religion: The Revelation of God as the Sublimation of Religion,* trans. Garrett Green (New York/London: T&T Clark, 2006). On Schmemann, see Thomas Hopko, "Two No's and One Yes," *St Vladimir's Theological Quarterly* 28 (1984), 45–48.

with very few exceptions, religious texts. They emanate from the Bible and from explicitly Christian liturgy, prayer, and meditation. We may accurately call them "sacred" or "spiritual" texts, but their sources lie within an unambiguously religious tradition.[4]

Spirituality

How, then, would we define spirit, spiritual, spirituality? Secular and religious people alike will often begin by asserting that "spirit" cannot be defined or pigeonholed. The ineffable, numinous, indescribable character of the spirit (or the Spirit) has not stopped many, whether religious or secular, from trying to describe it, often with abundant verbiage. But some of the most common and useful definitions of spirit are *apophatic*—meaning that they focus on what the spirit is *not*. Typical definitions of spirituality say that it speaks of the *im*-material, *un*-knowable, *in*-visible, *trans*-scendent. These lead in turn to the concept of the sacred, the holy, i.e., things that are *set apart* from the rest.[5]

---

[4]That tradition is Christian. Pärt draws deeply from the Christian West— mostly the Roman Catholic prayer and liturgical tradition that fed so much of the Western classical musical corpus—as well as from the Christian East. The "Christian East," often associated with the Orthodox churches, is broadly comprised of ecclesial communities that emerged from the Greek, Syriac, Armenian, Coptic, Ethiopian, and Georgian lands. The churches typically called "Orthodox" are rooted in the Middle East, North Africa, Asia Minor, Greece, Central and Eastern Europe, and Russia, with communities throughout the world.

[5]Among fundamental texts exploring this concept, see Mary Douglas, *Purity and Danger: An Analysis of Concepts of Pollution and Taboo* (London: Routledge, 1966), and Mircea Eliade, *The Sacred and the Profane: The Nature of Religion*, trans. Willard R. Trask (New York: Harcourt Brace, 1959), or perhaps more pertinently, Emil Durkheim, *The Elementary Forms*

The idea of spirituality as divorced from religion is relatively new.[6] Of itself, its novelty does not make it either a more or less valid concept, either an evolution toward enlightenment or a depraved shirking of fundamental human realities. But as a part of this development, spirituality has also become a more personal, less corporate affair. The word "spiritual" more often describes private (and subjective) experiences, in prayer, in the contemplation of nature, in practicing yoga, in experiencing art. The individual's experience of spirituality is perhaps one way of ensuring that the spirit is not overly defined or captured.[7] The less said about it the better—and attempts to harmonize mystical experience among groups of people are liable to squelch something that is best left unexpressed.

In that case, can religion even *be* spiritual? In the experience of much contemporary secular Western society, "religion"—even apart from the pejorative definitions of Barth and Schmemann— is the death of the spiritual: death by ossification (viz., theology), death by strangulation (viz., by politics and control, and the scandals that inevitably ensue). The leitmotif of religion—often broadly equated with "fundamentalism," through the semiotics of the cross, clerical collar, or monastic habit—as killer of spontaneity and purity runs so deep within popular culture that it has become cliché.[8] And yet "spiritual" and "religious" inevitably

---

of Religious Life, trans. Carol Edelman (Oxford: Oxford University Press, 2001).

[6] Here again see Taylor, *A Secular Age,* op. cit.

[7] For a darker interpretation of the private nature of spirituality, see Jeremy Carrette and Richard King, *Selling Spirituality: The Silent Takeover of Religion* (Abingdon, UK: Routledge, 2005).

[8] See, e.g., Peter E. Dans, *Christians in the Movies: A Century of Saints and Sinners* (New York: Rowmann & Littlefield, 2009).

overlap, in several ways. For most religious people the same transcendent, ineffable spirit ("God," perhaps) is the core of their faith and practice. There are also non-believers who are drawn specifically to overtly religious music, including Pärt's, because of its unique capacity to evoke "the numinous."[9] And there are non-practitioners who write stirring music to religious, liturgical texts. The understanding, experience, and configuration of "religion" and "spirituality" of Pärt's listeners vary a great deal, and we will be examining further below the relationship between the text, the composition, and the experience of the music.

And then there is Pärt himself. As I noted earlier, his compositions after 1976 are nearly all settings of sacred religious texts. It will become clear in the pages that follow that for him, the spiritual and the religious are organically integrated: neither is his religion a mere external symptom, nor is his spirituality unaffiliated. But first we will be considering the breadth and depth of Pärt's listenership itself, and how it came to be that way.

Pärt's Spiritual Reach: Critics and Artists

As a reader of this book you are no doubt aware of the unique place of Arvo Pärt within both high and popular culture. You are probably more than just aware of the "Arvo Pärt Phenomenon," you are likely a part of it. He and his music together are a force

[9]See the prologue, "What Is Religious Music?" to Wilfrid Mellers, *Celestial Music? Some Masterpieces of European Religious Music* (Woodbridge, UK: Boydell, 2002). xi–xv. Not a religious believer, Mellers has written an especially penetrating and theologically perceptive analysis of the *Passio*: "Arvo Pärt, God and Gospel: *Passio Domini Nostri Iesu Christi Secundum Iohannem* [Sic]," *Contemporary Music Review* 12, no. 2 (1995).

that bridges high and popular culture. Professional critics love or hate his work, but they rarely ignore it. When they are unfavorable it is often either because he is so widely popular (something classical music critics tolerate grudgingly if at all), or because they are unable to place him within their constructed narrative of twentieth-century music, or simply because he is overplayed. As to this last, it is not hard to feel that we have heard *Spiegel im Spiegel* in just about enough amateur and professional film soundtracks by now.[10] Far more significantly, and with no complaints from his listeners, Pärt has in recent years been tracked as the most-performed living composer in the world—more than Philip Glass, Steve Reich, John Adams, or Krzysztof Penderecki.[11] Of course, given how rarely contemporary composers are ever performed, it's not as if the world is experiencing an Arvo Pärt glut. Critics have found other reasons to be dismissive, and we will discuss these as well.

What interests us here is how Pärt's music—specifically his *tintin-nabuli* repertoire—speaks to listeners, and especially what strikes them as spiritual.[12] Of particular interest to me are all the non-religious people who find themselves moved spiritually by Pärt's work. This phenomenon is evident through the reactions of art-world personalities such as Michael Stipe, Thom Yorke, Björk, Jónsi Birgisson (of Sigur Rós), and Laurie Anderson. The breadth

[10]E.g., David Ng to Culture Monster, September 30, 2008, Samuel Wigley to Film Blog, May 29, 2008.

[11]http://bachtrack.com/top-ten-statistics-classical-music-2014.

[12]As we have noticed, the "spirituality" characterization applies almost exclusively to the *tintinnabuli* repertoire. His pre-1976 music is rarely associated with "spirituality" or, for that matter, with "silence." Although I do recall attending an ecumenical worship service in 1997 that employed Pärt's *Solfeggio* (1963).

of Pärt's reach as a harbinger of the spiritual is well attested. For example, Arthur Lubow remarks in the *New York Times*, "Many of Pärt's pieces are settings of religious texts, and even the instrumental works bear a whiff of church incense. Yet the compositions resonate profoundly for the unconverted as well as the faithful."[13] Audiences with a low tolerance for religion and its preachiness are liable to welcome this music for its ability to connect them with the transcendent. As another reviewer remarks:

> In this modern day and age, we shy away from discussing certain topics, such as religion. Arvo Pärt continues to speak about it for us in his music. What is most significant is that he does it without an agenda, without being pushy, often even without words, yet the meaning remains clear. Transcendence is possible, despite the fact that the shape it takes varies from individual to individual. Tonight, the chances are that we all experienced our own form of spiritual enlightenment, and not one walked away feeling indifferent.[14]

One hears a degree of surprise here that it is even possible to broach religious/spiritual topics without being a nuisance about it. Something of that surprise is registered by critic Wilfrid Mellers:

> One might have expected that the religious or numinous nature of Pärt's music would render it remote from most people in our age of unfaith. Such is not the case, for Pärt's innocence seems [. . .] hardly less relevant to what the Prayer Book calls 'men of good will.'[15]

---

[13]Arthur Lubow, "Arvo Pärt: The Sound of Spirit," *The New York Times Magazine*, October 15, 2010.

[14]Sasha Drozzina, "The Music of Arvo Pärt at Koerner Hall," http://bachtrack.com/review-toronto-arvo-part.

[15]Mellers, "Arvo Pärt, God and Gospel," 37f.

However startled such reviewers may be, Pärt's works often connect to the spiritual core of both the unconverted and the faithful. It may even be that he speaks in this way *more* clearly to those outside his faith tradition. Of all the literature on him only a small percentage is written from the explicit perspective of a believing Christian, still less an Orthodox Christian. Of the eleven honorary doctorates he has received to date, only one is from an Orthodox Christian institution.[16] True, church-affiliated choirs have embraced much of his repertoire, yet only a tiny number of these ensembles are dedicated to exploring the Orthodox musical inheritance, notable among them Cappella Romana.

Why is this so? I can only suggest some reasons. One may be that the spirituality of Pärt's work is obvious to a believing Christian, for whom the sacred texts speak for themselves as "spiritual." For such listeners, there is nothing there to excavate or to write about—it is plain. Other Christians, however, are uncomfortable with the way that Pärt has cast these very texts. To them, Pärt's "otherworldly" effect seems to them to belie Christianity's incarnational character. Jeremy Begbie has delivered a brief but influential critique of Pärt's music as creating the "contemplative ambience," of a "cool sonic cathedral." Begbie questions whether such an "escapist" ethos is true to the incarnation of Christ into real history and real suffering, on the cross.[17] We will have an opportunity below to explore further the effect of Pärt's music on people's perception of time. In the meantime, however incomplete

---

[16]St Vladimir's Orthodox Theological Seminary, in Yonkers, NY, awarded the Doctor of Music *honoris causa* on May 31, 2014.

[17]Jeremy S. Begbie, *Resounding Truth: Christian Wisdom in the World of Music*, Engaging Culture (Grand Rapids, MI: Baker Academic, 2007), 261; see also pp. 223f.

this assessment may feel, the evident fact is that Pärt leaves some Christians cold.[18]

The reactions of the non-Christian, the non-religious, the nominally religious, the atheist, are of particular interest given that Pärt himself is, unlike them, grounded in religious faith and draws on religious texts that he feels are spiritual masterpieces. Which, as we saw, people find surprising. So: what comes across as "spiritual?" Why is it that an atheist friend tells me that when she listens to Pärt she turns out all the lights and lies on the floor, sometimes in tears? Why do we read on social media things like, "I am not a religious person. I have always said though, that if there is anything that could possibly make me so, it would be Pärt's music"?

Here are some of the words that come up most frequently within social media, when asked the question of what makes Pärt's music spiritual: pure, honest, simple, essential, transparent. Then there are words like: angelic, oceanic, contemplative, reflective, mystical, ethereal, transcendent. These latter adjectives are more directly evocative of "spirituality," but they depend, in some way, on the former.[19] It is because the music is pure, honest, and reductive that

---

[18]Begbie, along with several other critics, groups Pärt together with John Tavener and Henryk Górecki—a common practice that is rarely useful. While Begbie qualifies his inclusion of Pärt in that category, these three composers are lumped together as "holy minimalists," a convenient but facile characterization that fails to do justice either to the differences between them, or to the broad scope of their work. A case in point (with a telling title), is Josiah Fisk, "The New Simplicity: The Music of Górecki, Tavener, and Pärt," *The Hudson Review* 47, no. 3 (1994).

[19]There is a Russian saying that expresses the correlation of the simple and angelic: Где просто—там ангелов со сто, а где мудрено—там ни одного. "Where there is simplicity, there are hundreds of angels. Where there is clev-

it manages to induce contemplation, and a sense of something greater than ourselves.

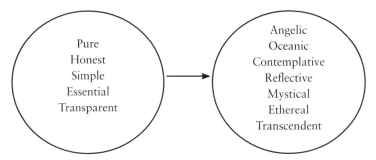

Timelessness and Time, Transcendence and Engagement

In so far as the word "transcendent" speaks to being taken outside or beyond oneself, it bespeaks an altered relationship to time. If Pärt's work can be evocative of a "sonic cathedral"—and there is nothing wrong or antithetical to Christianity in a sonic cathedral—this could be part of how *tintinnabuli* works. Its groundedness in the triad means that the music will often gravitate powerfully toward single, sustained tonal centers, sometimes underscored by a drone.[20] Added to the reductive character of his work, these factors make it so that some of his compositions approach an almost ambient quality. Ambient but engaged. Outside time but emphatically incarnated.[21]

erness, there isn't one." Arvo Pärt refers to this aphorism in Jordi Savall, "A Conversation with Arvo Pärt," *Music and Literature* 1, no. 1 (2012), 12.

[20]Drones feature, for example, in portions of *Te Deum, Kanon Pokajanen*, and *Fratres* in some orchestrations.

[21]See Ivan Moody, *Modernism and Orthodox Spirituality in Contemporary Music* (Joensuu, Finland: International Society for Orthodox Church Music, 2014), which speaks specifically to "the very incarnate nature of the 'spiritual' in Arvo Pärt's Music" (pp. 184f.).

If the ambient or timeless character of Pärt's work can be explained musically, so can its incarnate character, as I will be doing below.[22] But this same quality of embodiment—the antithesis of cold detachment—is also demonstrated by how Pärt's music reaches those who suffer, something we will discuss further below. People in situations of pain, people on their journey toward death, often find a curiously *empathetic* quality in Pärt's work: they feel that the music is suffering with them. Far from standing outside of human realities in some far-removed and uninvolved stratum, the music is embodied in time and space, and in the human heart. The music can evoke in listeners a sense of the tension between time and eternity. We are reminded that no one can experience the transcendent but through the immanent. The eternal Word becomes flesh, else we would not know it. And if icons are "windows into heaven" they must first be wood and paint. Space-time and eternity are always together, in a holy tension—and this is what Pärt is after: "That is my goal: time and timelessness are connected. This instant and eternity are struggling within us."[23]

The ahistorical character of Pärt's music has elicited a further criticism: that the composer has unacceptably dissociated himself from the inexorable trajectory of contemporary music history.[24] It is as if timelessness is an ideological stance, over and against a quasi-Hegelian notion of artistic progress. The inability to place Pärt within the perceived history of twentieth-century music leads critics to create artificial new categories—"Holy Minimalism" or

[22]See at pp. 40–43, and at 176–86.

[23]Liner notes, *Tabula Rasa* (ECM 1275, 1984).

[24]See David Clarke, "Parting Glances: Aesthetic Solace or Act of Complicity?," *Musical Times* 134, no. 1810 (1993). The deep investment in a constructed portraiture of music history seems to make some forget simply to listen.

"The New Simplicity"—together (inevitably) with John Tavener and Henryk Górecki. A more favorable interpretation of the same effect comes from Alex Ross, who points out in the *New Yorker* that Pärt's work is at once familiar but "does not duplicate the music of the past." Ross is one critic who, though fully cognizant of twentieth-century music history, avoids forcing composers into his portraiture of it. He also immediately addresses the "cool detachment" critique: Pärt's music, says Ross, manages to "obliterate the rigidities of space and time." But the effect of that transcendence is such that it "binds the mind to *an eternal present.*"[25]

It sometimes feels as if much of the appraisal of Pärt's work is the result of a difficulty in understanding how something can be at once detached and at the same time deeply engaged. Not of the world but emphatically in it; transcendent yet immanent. I imagine that a Buddhist sensibility would embrace this paradox immediately. So would a Christian: this, after all, is precisely what the Incarnation is all about.

Clearing Clutter: Feel the World Stand Still

In a *tour de force* essay that spans Otis Redding, Led Zeppelin, The Beatles, and Funkadelic, music writer Rick Moody assesses Arvo Pärt. Listening to the *Tabula Rasa* CD, which features the eponymous composition as well as *Fratres* and *Cantus*, he describes the music as "frankly spiritual and completely tonal."

> For these reasons, and because the pieces are *so* simple, there is some grumbling in classical music circles about Pärt's work. He's not serious, he's conservative, etc.

[25]Alex Ross, "Consolations: The Uncanny Voice of Arvo Pärt," *The New Yorker*, December 2 2002, emphasis added.

I didn't care about any of this when I first heard these record-ings, and I still don't. Pärt's compositions split me open like I was an oyster, and the way they did it was by exploiting the simple harmonies of ancient western music, the kind of dignity and stateliness that I associated with the music of the church as I first heard it. I can't fully explain what it is about this simplicity and tonality that was so moving to me. And I'm not sure I want to.[26]

Many have joined Moody in observing that Pärt's music bears the promise of simplicity, purity, and silence. These qualities have a way of exposing one's inner life, and that is partly because they clear the clutter. They are an antidote to a culture that is complex, sullied, and noisy. This "stilling" aspect of his work has been particularly resonant within the alternative contempo-rary music scene. Pärt's music makes one "feel the world stand still," said an Estonian folktronic artist, to the composer's warm acclaim.[27] Such stillness is readily associated with a purgative, if not cathartic aspect of spirituality, in contrast to the world's din, ". . . a cleansing of all the noise that surrounds us,"[28] as well as our own inner noise: "His chords silence the noise of the self."[29] Several contemporary bands who cite Pärt as a major influence, such as Sigur Rós, Stars of the Lid, Sunn O))), and Mogwai, find their work characterized by the same words used to describe his. Sample comments about these bands on social media frequently

[26]Rick Moody, *On Celestial Music, and Other Adventures in Listening* (New York: Little, Brown & Co, 2012), 278.

[27]See Siim Nestor, "Arvo Pärt: 'Ju me siis salaja . . .'," *Eesti Ekspress,* Sep-tember 11, 2010.

[28]The oft-cited quotation of Gidon Kremer, from the *Tabula Rasa* liner notes (ECM 1275, 1984).

[29]Again Ross, "Consolations: The Uncanny Voice of Arvo Pärt."

tend toward the spiritual: "Sublime." "Heaven." "Thank you for the blessing." "A true vision." "A gateway to the soul." "This makes me fly." It is no coincidence that these bands are largely drone-based ambient artists—their music, though deeply layered, is repetitive, and . . . simple. Their work plays with time, seeming to go outside it. Pärt even remarked, on hearing Sunn O))), "It makes time stop, time in big blocks."[30]

A significant variety of artists—photographers, choreographers, sculptors, painters, writers, artisans—have spoken of the effect of Pärt's music on their work. Pärt's music plays as they create, write, sculpt, dance. It is not simply a matter of establishing an ambience—though there are critics who relegate it to insubstantial background music, "a higher Muzak for sensitive souls."[31] It is the ability of this music to instill tranquility. Having gone through its own process of purgative reduction, the music has the effect of expurgating the inessential. Here are comments from social media, specifically by artists who listen to Pärt:

- "It aligns my soul."
- "I've always tried to imbue my work with the kind of quietness, if not silence, that I get from Arvo's music—sculpting about silence."
- "The scraping noise of this world becomes quiet and I can actually hear the stories and see the images in all their color and subtlety."
- "His work establishes for me some continuity between the world in my head and the one I feel outside it. This helps create a context in which creative acts are more possible."

---

[30]Siim Nestor, op. cit.
[31]Referred to in Ross, "Consolations: The Uncanny Voice of Arvo Pärt."

- "The effect is paradoxical. I have to be careful because the music is so astoundingly beautiful that my own piddling efforts seem unspeakably paltry and small in comparison. But the music also serves as a touchstone to remind me, during times of self-doubt and self-criticism, that the creative process is something transcendent and magisterial, something that connects me, in some ineffable way, with other artists. Listening to Pärt while immersed in the solitary act of writing makes me feel less . . . alone."

It is not only a matter of clearing the mental cache. As this last comment demonstrates, the music has a way of connecting people to something. There is a presence to be felt, one that evidently has a particular resonance, as we shall see below, for those who are suffering.

Spirituality, Empathy, and Hope

When we think of "those who are suffering" we may have in mind people in situations of extreme distress, experiencing severe grief, the imprisoned, the dying. But in different ways and to different extents, *everyone* in this world, without exception, suffers. The world is broken and no-one is exempt from the resulting tremors of pain, loss, incompleteness. The effect of Pärt's music on "the suffering" has the potential therefore to be felt universally. Having said that, the particular relationship between this music and those who are in acute states of suffering or in the process of dying is observed with increasing frequency. Alex Ross's *New Yorker* article, "Consolations: The Uncanny Voice of Arvo Pärt," drew attention to the phenomenon relatively early.[32] Ross describes

[32]Ibid.

encounter after encounter with people who were in distress and/ or dying, at hospices, at centers for AIDS victims, who wanted to hear only Pärt's music. "One or two such anecdotes seem sentimental; a series of them begins to suggest a slightly uncanny phenomenon," he writes. And lo, one of my close colleagues just recently told me of her late sister who, unprompted by anything she'd read on the subject, listened constantly and exclusively to Pärt during the last months of her battle with cancer. His music's effect on the anguished has quietly become something of a phenomenon, and has found its way into popular culture.[33]

Tending as it does toward minor-key tonalities and moderate tempos, Pärt's music is often experienced as "sad."[34] Its heartbreaking character, however, tends to attract rather than repel. That Pärt's music, in its sorrow, is a source of solace or consolation is one of its more significant, if mystifying gifts. This quality is another part of the "spiritual" puzzle—how it allows people to experience hope and transcendence. But, as mentioned earlier, the first-felt effect of Pärt's work upon those who suffer, even before consolation or hope, is *empathy*. Many listeners do not return to this music to disappear into a "sonic cathedral." They return because they feel heard and accompanied in their suffering; the

[33] "Rectify," an American drama series on cable television about a wrongly-convicted man freed after serving nineteen years on death row, featured an evocative use of "Silentium" from *Tabula Rasa*. A chaplain plays the piece on a tape-recorder for the man during his solitary confinement, to transformative effect. Season 2, episode 6: "Mazel Tov," scene beginning at 40:39.

[34] The National Public Radio blog "Deceptive Cadence," in an entry called "The Saddest Music In The World: 6 Tunes To Make You Teary-Eyed," listed *Cantus in Memory of Benjamin Britten* among the six. (http://www.npr. org/blogs/deceptivecadence/2010/09/27/130157375/the-saddest-music-in-the-world-7-tunes-to-make-you-tear-up).

music meets them in their affliction. People in their darker hours do not, in the first instance, want to be "cheered up." They want to be understood for their suffering. Art is capable of expressing the depths of their feeling, often perhaps better than they can themselves.

As if to prove my point, the following comment has just now appeared on the Arvo Pärt Project Facebook page. I reproduce it in its entirety:

> I have an ally, which accompanied me upwards to my supreme spiritual moments, then, was with me on the horrific descent into suffering, death, and crisis, then, once again upwards, then, once again downwards in the perpetual juxtaposing of the polar opposites. The name of my ally is Tabula Rasa, through it, I came to know of a transcendent perspective; Fratres being the final decree of the reality inherent in the center of my soul.

There is evidently something therapeutic in hearing one's feelings expressed musically—this is what draws people to music of sadness and of anger, to poignant ballads and to heavy metal. Seeking out music that will speak to us and speak *for* us is but part of the story. It is an important part—for a great deal of the consolation experienced by Pärt's audience comes purely by virtue of the assurance that someone else has an inkling, or maybe even a deeper knowledge, of what they are going through. The consolation of Pärt's work goes deeper. The mystery is that it does not stop at sadness: embedded within it, inextricably woven into it, is a voice of genuine hope. Not a facile, cheery hope, but one that knows well the depths of despair, and knows that there is a way through it.

The "bright sadness" of this book's third section will be devoted largely to this phenomenon, for it is a major factor in the power of this particular music—a spiritual power that draws on an experience both lived and prayed. There, the links between suffering and consolation—already intuited by listeners—will be explored further, with both a theological and musicological focus.

"Monkish Mystic:" Constructing the Pärt Persona

The actual sound of Pärt's music and its effect on its listeners rarely exists in isolation from an image of the composer as monk, mystic, recluse—all serving to enhance the overall ethos of "spirituality." It is partly a self-propagating impression that also gets a push once in a while, for the monkish image also has its roots in some factors that make it rather easy to promote. There is the music itself, whose most oft-reproduced fragments do sound ethereal in a way that is evocative of prayer. Pärt's religious tradition can seem colorful, not for its Christianity as such but for its Eastern ethos. There is Pärt's reticence—his reluctance to say or write very much publically—which tends only to intensify people's sense of mystery about him. And there is, yes, the beard. A relatively long one. The press began commenting on it as soon as Pärt arrived in Western Europe. Nora Pärt remarks:

> When we came to the West, Arvo was a real gift to the media. It was such a gratifying topic to report about: an exotic being, mystic, monk, beard, medieval vocabulary, detached from the world, etc.

Here the composer himself chimes in: "Some people even thought I wore a false beard!"[35]

[35]Leopold Brauneiss, Enzo Restagno, Saale Kareda, Arvo Pärt, *Arvo Pärt in*

Matters approaching religion and spirituality are by nature notoriously difficult for the media to get right; such subjects too easily lend themselves to facile characterizations that fail to do justice to inner realities. Upon his appearance on the wider cultural scene in the 1980s, it was inevitable that Arvo Pärt's provenance and appearance were easily seized upon in the press, sometimes favorably and sometimes not, as arcane and mystical. "The idea that within the field of spirituality there can also exist a normality and naturalness that doesn't land immediately in the realms of mysticism was obviously quite foreign to the general public," Nora continues. The idea that Arvo Pärt, while a serious Christian believer who reverently reads the ancient ascetical writers, is also a normal, friendly-though-introverted person with a family and a car and a wry sense of humor, finds no traction in the media or in popular culture. Normalcy makes poor copy.

Critics and commentators then struggle to slot Pärt into one or another spiritual-*cum*-cultural category, or attempt—sometimes even successfully—to say something credible about the Orthodox tradition. A good example can be found in a sentence by Wolfgang Sandner that surely sent many readers to their dictionaries when he likened Pärt's compositions to "the hesychastic prayers of a musical anchorite."[36] And then, on the level of the absurd, there is the painting of Arvo Pärt in the style of an Orthodox icon, complete with halo, not—one hopes—in order to make him an object of veneration, but perhaps in a winking recognition of his effect on some of his fans, and of the image that has been propagated, sometimes consciously cultivated.

Conversation, trans. Robert Crow (Champaign, IL: Dalkey Archive, 2012). (henceforth, "Restagno"), 62.
[36]Liner notes, *Tabula Rasa* (ECM 1275, 1984).

A word is due here about the role of ECM records in the hearing, understanding, and dissemination of Pärt's music. It would be impossible to overstate the role of ECM's founder and director, Manfred Eicher, in all of these crucial roles. When Manfred first heard *Tabula Rasa* in his car, as the story is often told, he had to pull over, find better reception, and listen to the piece to its conclusion. From that moment he sought out the composer, inaugurating a cherished artistic relationship and friendship that has truly shaped the musical landscape of its time. Eicher's ear for the art of music, and his gift for discovery, production, and dissemination of music, is justly renowned. So is ECM's musical and also visual esthetic. ECM's spare, reductive visual style, itself the subject of several books,[37] predates the record company's relationship with Pärt. So does its slogan, so appropriate to the composer: "The Next Best Sound to Silence." ECM has by now released over sixteen hundred records, united in their album art by an absence of clutter, a reduction to essentials. The relationship between Eicher/ECM—predisposed to deep listening, a preternaturally fine-tuned artistic sensibility, an alertness to silence and purity—and Arvo Pärt is a match made in heaven.

It would be misleading to suggest that ECM consciously propagated a "mystical" image for Pärt. Laura Dolp observes in an essay, referring to the accompanying material to *Passio*, "every aspect of its design supports the image of Pärt as a pious, solitary spiritual seeker who lives in the embodied moment."[38] But since ECM's

---

[37]See, e.g., Lars Müller, *ECM: Sleeves of Desire: A Cover Story* (Princeton: Princeton Architectural Press, 1996); *Windfall Light: The Visual Language of ECM* (Zürich: Lars Müller Publishers, 2010).

[38]Laura Dolp, "Arvo Pärt in the Marketplace," in *The Cambridge Companion to Arvo Pärt*, ed. Andrew Shenton (Cambridge: Cambridge University Press, 2012), 185.

aesthetics and production values effectively convey an image of purity and mystic transcendence for virtually *all* of its artists, I would suggest rather that a confluence of factors—ECM's ascetic ethos, the way Pärt looks and the way his music sounds—has managed unwittingly to compound an image that others have constructed in a more intentional way, often through mention of his Orthodox Christian faith.

The evident fact of Pärt's affiliation with the Orthodox Church bears mention in the context of the media discussion, because "Eastern Orthodoxy" has its own somewhat esoteric image, at least in the West. Western (Protestant, Catholic) Christianity does not enjoy a great spiritual allure among the kind of crossover audiences attracted to Pärt. Eastern Orthodoxy, on the other hand, seems to be just foreign enough, inscrutable enough, and exotic enough to carry a whiff of mystery. It is the aroma of The East, a hemisphere that seems to bespeak "mysticism" to the Western mind.[39] Descriptives like "hesychast," "anchorite," and inevitable allusions to icons—all associated with Orthodoxy—accumulate to contribute significantly to Pärt's spiritual persona.

That being said, Pärt's "monkish" image is not an *ex nihilo* construct. The Orthodox Church arguably does privilege the mystical and the monastic in its theology and practice more than do

[39]The insights on this score of Edward Said in *Orientalism* (Penguin, 1978) have been applied to Eastern Orthodox Christianity, e.g. in essays such as Christopher D.L. Johnson, "'He Has Made the Dry Bones Live': Orientalism's Attempted Resuscitation of Eastern Christianity," *Journal of the American Academy of Religion* 82, no. 3 (2014). Orthodox Christians have frequently been complicit in the construction of an identity as "Eastern," in contrast to the "West." See George Demacopoulos and Aristotle Papanikolaou, ed. *Orthodox Constructions of the West*, Orthodox Christianity and Contemporary Thought (New York: Fordham University Press, 2013).

Western Christian traditions. And Pärt is a believing Orthodox Christian who goes to church, frequents monasteries, and lives, reads, and prays that tradition. He sets his music to sacred texts that he says carry the deepest meaning to him. He is known to speak of his music in explicitly spiritual terms. The image of Pärt as reclusive mystical monastic is, in the end, a portraiture distorted by imbalance, one that has enabled listeners and critics to "place" him, perhaps to pigeonhole him, and certainly to exoticize him—as people are wont to do with complex, subtle realities, especially spiritual ones. Let us give Pärt the last word here:

> I am not a prophet, not a cardinal, not a monk. I am not even a vegetarian. Don't be confused by cheap tabloid information. Of course I am in monasteries more often than in concert halls—but then again, you have no idea how many times I am in concert halls.[40]

The Way to Orthodoxy

Having qualified the spiritualized image, we can say a few things about Pärt's actual relationship with the Orthodox Church, beginning with his way into it. The journey took place during his years of pivotal transition, marked by a near-silence in compositional output. As we will be seeing in the next section of this book, several elements conspired to make that period formative, both musically and spiritually. There was the musical search through monody and early music, there were the spiritual texts that were finding their way into his hands during the early 70s, and there was Nora, whom he would marry in 1972, whose influence and

[40]"Background Information" to *Litany* (ECM 1592, 1996), online at http://ecmrecords.com/Background/Background_1592.php

accompaniment in his life is inestimable, and whose support and comprehension of the totality of his life and work—to this day—is likewise incalculable.

Pärt joined the Orthodox Church in 1972, almost concurrently with Nora, though each arrived by a separate path. Born to an Orthodox father and a Lutheran mother, baptized and raised Protestant, Pärt did not feel particularly religious in his youth. It was in the conservatory that, studying Western composers' settings of sacred texts, he began to take interest in their spiritual content.

His awakened interest in the Christian faith took a definitive turn as he entered his "silent" period. Significantly, the texts and music that informed his journey in the course of this period were almost exclusively sacred in their character. The texts that inspired him to fill his notebooks with monophonic melodies were preeminently the Psalms. The music he was listening to, that would inspire his commitment to purity and reduction, was likewise sacred: Ockeghem, Josquin, Dufay, Palestrina, and of course Gregorian chant. Furthermore, these discoveries entailed developments in his inner life that went beyond the music. For he began to realize that one cannot truly apprehend the depth of Gregorian chant or of other sacred music without taking a fuller account of its spiritual character, specifically its rootedness in *prayer*. As a result he sought to understand and in some way to enter into the ascetical ethos and faith out of which that music came. For Pärt, that meant that the genuine reception of this music was dependent on one thing alone:

> Only through prayer is it possible. If you have prayer in your hand, like a flashlight, with this light you see what's there.

It all depends on you yourself. This language of prayer is a foreign language. If you know even a little of it, the material that is in this language will be a bit more understandable to you. And that begins a kind of mutual exchange. It feeds you, and opens your eyes. And it becomes a measuring stick for everything.[41]

So Pärt's journey toward a deepened Christian faith, and eventually into the Orthodox Church, was thoroughly intertwined with his musical odyssey. As for what he was reading at the time, Pärt mentions several books that were most significant to him, among them *The Imitation of Christ* by Thomas à Kempis—a text that he transcribed in its entirety by hand.[42] During this time he also began reading the *Philokalia*, a multivolume anthology of Eastern Christian ascetical texts. Later on, after his reception into Orthodoxy, he began reading more and more of the Church Fathers, mostly the ancients (Dorotheos of Gaza, the *Ladder of Divine Ascent* by St John Climacus) but also the twentieth-century Silouan of Mount Athos. The texts of that great *staretz* would undergird some of Pärt's later compositions, and Silouan's spiritual son, Archimandrite Sophrony (Sakharov), would later come to influence him to an immeasurable degree.

So it came to be that in the early 1970s Arvo Pärt became acquainted with a certain Orthodox priest in Tallinn. During this same time period he met Nora, who—through the same priest—would herself join the Orthodox Church. Within three months of Nora's baptism, Arvo was received into the Orthodox Church.

---

[41]In Peter C. Bouteneff, Recorded Interview with Arvo and Nora Pärt (Laulasmaa, Estonia: unpublished, 2014).

[42]Ibid.

Two more factors, which I will only mention briefly, help fill out the picture of Pärt's Orthodoxy. One is that, although the texts, liturgy, and prayer life of the Orthodox Church are what courses through his spiritual veins, Arvo Pärt is a deeply ecumenical person, the antithesis of an Orthodox zealot or exclusivist. It is after all the *Western* sacred musical tradition that is his primary musical influence, and the spiritual tradition it comes from carries deep meaning for him. At first, the texts he set to music came almost exclusively from the Roman Catholic tradition, or simply from the Bible; only in 1989 did he begin to set texts from the Orthodox prayer tradition and from the writings of St Silouan.[43]

The other factor I would mention is the complex Estonian religious and national context. The second half of the twentieth century was a period of painful turmoil for a nation moving toward independence while under Soviet occupation. These political realities carried significant religious implications. The atheist regime eroded the religion of a formerly far more devout Estonia, such that joining a church, declaring oneself "religious" during the occupation was seen as a dissident act. This meant that Pärt's conversion in the 1970s only added to his disfavor in the eyes of the government. Add to this that anti-Soviet sentiment sometimes spilled over into anti-Russian feelings, and although Pärt himself never understood his affiliation with Orthodoxy in any national sense, some indicted him for joining a "Russian" church. But his decision was considered an act of courage by many who kept their own religious faith secret.

Since Estonian independence in 1991 there has been much healing, both religious and national. Religious adherents are still

---

[43]On the texts and their ecclesiastical provenance, see below, from the next subheading.

a minority in Estonia but they exercise their faith in freedom. The Pärts were able to repatriate to Estonia after more than two decades in Berlin, and Arvo Pärt had already in the early 1990s re-forged close relationships with the Estonian music world, notably through Tõnu Kaljuste, the Tallinn Chamber Orchestra, and the Estonian Philharmonic Chamber Choir, who have become among his preeminent interpreters in recordings and concerts.

Orthodoxy in the Music: Text Settings

As I have noted, Pärt's musical influences are chiefly Western European. The sacred texts that have undergirded most of his works, especially up until 1990, have tended toward either scriptural passages—common to all Christian expressions—or to Western Christian liturgical texts and prayers. In recent decades he has increasingly used texts particular to the Eastern Orthodox tradition. In 1984 we can see the first hint of acknowledgment of his Russian/Orthodox identity with the composition *Zwei slawische Psalmen,* his first work in Church Slavonic.[44] This was but a hint of what would come in the 1990s, a decade whose compositions are textually dominated by the Orthodox Christian tradition, with a leaning toward the Church Slavonic language. In 1990 he composed *Bogoroditse Djevo,* a boisterous setting of the hymn to Mother of God, also in Church Slavonic and leaning—uncharacteristically—in the sonic direction of Russian Orthodox singing. 1991 saw the composition of *Silouan's Song,* set to a text by the twentieth century Russian Athonite monk Silouan,

---

[44]Church Slavonic was a language developed specifically for liturgical use in the Orthodox Church. See А. Г. Кравецкий, А. А. Плетнева, *История церковнославянского языка в России (Конец XIX–XX Века)* (Moscow, 2001: Языки русской культуры).

whose legacy is lived in the monastic community in Essex, UK, with which Pärt is closely affiliated. *Trisagion* (1992) is set to the introductory sequence of Orthodox prayers. *Litany* (1994) is a series of short prayers by fifth-century St John Chrysostom for each hour of the day. Then there is the *Canon of Repentance to Our Lord Jesus Christ*, attributed to the eighth-century St Andrew of Crete. Portions of this text (always in Church Slavonic) are the basis of several shorter works: *Ninye k Vam* (1989), *Memento* (1994), *Für Lennart in Memoriam* (2006).[45] In its complete setting, *Kanon Pokajanen* (1997) is one of Pärt's extended masterpieces. *Triodion* (1998) and *Lamentate* (2002) are settings of traditional Orthodox prayers. *Orient/Occident* (2000) is written to the Nicene Creed in Church Slavonic. The *Canon to the Guardian Angel*, like the *Canon of Repentance*, undergirds more than one composition: *These Words* (2008) and Symphony No. 4 "Los Angeles" (2008).[46]

We come finally to Pärt's most recent "large work," *Adam's Lament* (2010). It would be difficult to overstate the importance of this piece, not only musically but within Pärt's spiritual life. As just noted, since the late 1980s he has been close to the community founded by the Archimandrite Sophrony (+1993), spiritual son of St Silouan the Athonite. "Adam's Lament" is St Silouan's meditation giving word to Adam's feeling of grief, loss, and repentance upon losing the grace of the Holy Spirit.[47] The theme of

---

[45]The church hymn used here is in fact the heirmos of a pre-existing canon, one that is sung at Orthodox funeral and memorial services: the Resurrection Octoechos Canon in Tone 6. That canon in turn forms the backbone of the Canon of Repentance.

[46]The texts in several of the compositions mentioned above are articulated instrumentally, but not sung. See below at pp. 75–78.

[47]The complete text may be found below in Appendix III.

"God-forsakenness," a disposition of mourning, hope, and fervent supplication to God, ran deeply in Silouan's thought and that of Sophrony as well.[48] It is unquestionably characteristic of Pärt's work as a whole, and his organic affiliation with Sophrony's monastic community in England runs deep. The text of "Adam's Lament" had accompanied Pärt for decades as he strove to set it to music—he finally limited himself to its opening section for his composition, completed in 2010. If all of Pärt's compositions allow a glimpse into his soul, no doubt *Adam's Lament* does so to an exceptional extent.

Arvo Pärt's chosen musical settings testify to the ecumenical nature of his Christian faith and identity. Unlike some, he does not affiliate himself to Eastern Orthodoxy with the kind of impassioned devotion one might have for a nation or a football team. Orthodoxy is where he resides spiritually. But his reverence for the Western musical tradition, itself so inextricably bound with the Western religious tradition, runs deep. So does his ability to recognize genuine Christian faith and life outside the geographical and canonical bounds of Orthodoxy. It took Pärt more than a decade after his 1976 *tintinnabuli* watershed to begin giving musical expression to the Orthodox world in which he was personally immersed. Once he did so, the texts from both Eastern and Western Christian spiritual legacies would emerge in turns, as they do to the present day. Pärt is a man who in his spiritual life is both grounded and free.

---

[48]This theme will be explored more thoroughly below, in the book's next section, at pp. 171–76.

Orthodoxy in the Music: Preliminary Explorations

I commented above on the Eastern mystique associated with the Orthodox Church. A few authors have begun to try to make deeper connections between Pärt's music and his spirituality. Several seek insight from Orthodox theology and liturgy, dwelling, naturally, on the features most commonly associated with the Orthodox Church—icons, liturgical chant, and sometimes, bells. Each of these connections makes a degree of sense but rarely goes beneath the surface. One can make some fruitful connections between Pärt's music and icons: both are typically reductive in style and ideally transparent to their subject. Icons are not themselves subjects of worship; they are depictions, or translations, of the divine and heavenly realities they depict. Pärt would likely feel comfortable with such an association, seeing his own music as "mere translations" of the sacred texts that underlie it. Paul Hillier takes up these kinds of ideas, also making an entirely viable connection between the strict patterns and rules that govern the painting of an icon—with the goal of a more faithful depiction of the transcendent—and the rules and patterns deployed by Pärt to the same ends.[49]

As for Orthodox liturgical chant and choral singing, these have not been a serious influence on Pärt's compositions; the composer himself frequently and strenuously rejects the notion that they are. Yet the matter is possibly more intricate than he allows. When one hears strains of Russian Church music in pieces like *Silouan's Song,* or *Kanon Pokajanen,* (often under the sway of the language of these compositions' respective texts), it is undoubtedly at least the influence of *Russian music* writ large. On the other hand, can

[49]Hillier, *Arvo Pärt,* 3–5.

Russian Orthodox church music really be dissociated from the Russian musical tradition? There are deep veins of connection, even if they are neither necessarily direct, clear, or consistent. And naturally, the Russian (and dare I say, Russian-Orthodox) influences are more prominent in compositions set to texts in Russian or Slavonic.[50]

As for the influence of Byzantine (Orthodox) chant, which is frequently sung with a drone (*ison* or *isokratema*): a few of Pärt's compositions employ a drone voice, such as in the *Te Deum* (1985). That piece is sung over a recorded wind-harp that Pärt has himself related to the Byzantine chant.[51] Otherwise, as far as the composer himself is concerned, he is on record, clearly and consistently, that the sacred/liturgical music that has in fact influenced him is that of the West, not the East.[52] Having myself heard, sung, and conducted Orthodox Church music—mostly of the Slavic tradition—throughout my life, his assertion rings true, as qualified above.

Then there are the bells, which are at the explicit heart of *tintinnabuli* ("little bells"). The Orthodox Church, especially in

[50]See below at pp. 78–80.

[51]Ivan Moody likens the sustained notes in *Litany* to the *ison* as well. See Moody, *Modernism and Orthodox Spirituality in Contemporary Music*, 182.

[52]In a recorded interview before a concert at the Metropolitan Museum of Art in New York, June 2, 2014, Pärt said, "The liturgical life of the Orthodox Church is rich, and it feeds all the human senses. But my musical education was formed mostly on the basis of Roman Catholic church music. The Orthodox faith came to me later, and not so much through the music of the church, but through the teachings and words of early Christianity, and Byzantine holy men. And that spiritual heritage has influenced me greatly." http://www.metmuseum.org/events/programs/concerts-and-performances/live-stream/2014/arvo-part. See also Restagno, 36.

some localities, does place special emphasis on the practice of bell-ringing (as do some Western churches with deep and living traditions of campanology). The Orthodox, as is their wont, carefully categorize, regulate, and even theologize bell-ringing, but never seem to lose sight of the basic sonic beauty and its role in worship. But the *tintinnabuli* style/ethos/world arises out of its own origins that have nothing to do with the Orthodox approach to bells. The name arose as a descriptive: this is how the music *sounded*, once the triad-voice and the melody-voice came together in their indissoluble union. Arvo, and Nora (who came up with the *tintinnabuli* name), caution against taking the bell connection too literally: "it is a metaphor . . . it is poetical."[53] There are several evocative deployments of actual bells in Pärt's repertoire, for instance in *Miserere* (1989), *Litany* (1994), *Beatus Petronius* (2011 version), and perhaps most famously *Cantus* (1977). The prepared piano in *Tabula Rasa* (1977) also sounds bell-like, as does, in another way, the bass section in the final measures of *Nunc Dimittis* (2001). But I am not sure how much more there is to say in direct connection with the Orthodox Church's use or "theology" of bells. Paul Hillier, again, yields several insightful observations on bells in Pärt's work, and on the role of bells in Orthodoxy.[54] But is there a genuine correlation between the two? An essay by Marguerite Bostonia, provides useful information about bells in Orthodoxy, and insightfully analyzes some of the specific ways in which *tintinnabuli* evokes them.[55] That evocation is undeniable, but its

[53]Lubow, "Arvo Pärt: The Sound of Spirit."

[54]*Arvo Pärt*, 18–23.

[55]Marguerite Bostonia, "Bells as Inspiration for Tintinnabulation," in *The Cambridge Companion to Arvo Pärt*, ed. Andrew Shenton (Cambridge: Cambridge University Press, 2012), 128–139.

basis specifically in Orthodox Christian approaches to the bell remains for me hypothetical and unconvincing.

It is only appropriate to want to explore Pärt's music in terms of his church affiliation as these writers have, and in so doing, to look first to the most evident features of Orthodox Christianity. The process has to start somewhere, and it has been good to see some very recent and insightful attempts to go still further beyond the surface.[56] With the present book I am attempting to build on the foundations laid so far. As a part of that process, I will now devote some sustained attention next to something that Pärt identifies as the very ground of his music, and which surely holds a vital key to its spiritual character.

The Role of the Text

When considering what gives Pärt's music its spiritual life, one of the answers may be either glaringly obvious or curiously hidden: the texts. Of his nearly 90 distinct compositions since 1976 to the time of this writing there are very few that are not set to a text, and specifically a *sacred* text—i.e., taken either from the Bible or from Christian prayers, liturgies, or writings. To a person conversant with biblical, liturgical, and/or theological themes, locating the spirituality in Pärt's music requires no great excavation: it is right there in the words, addressed to God, to Jesus, to Mary or another saint. Yet, apart from categorizing Pärt as either a "sacred composer" or (perhaps more pejoratively) a "holy minimalist,"

---

[56]See, e.g., Toomas Siitan's introduction to Kristina Kõrver, Kai Kutman, Hedi Rosma, eds. *In Principio: The Word in Arvo Pärt's Music* (Laulasmaa, Estonia: Arvo Pärt Centre, 2014), and the chapter on Arvo Pärt in Moody, *Modernism and Orthodox Spirituality in Contemporary Music*, op. cit.

the basis of his texts in sacred traditions receives little or no attention in existing studies of the spirituality of his work.[57] I suggest that the reasons are to be found within the following two areas: 1) the relationship between the spiritual and the religious,[58] and 2) the relationship between text and music. Neither of these relationships are straightforward.

The first issue is that the religious texts to which Pärt sets his music and the themes that inform them do not carry a spiritual resonance for everyone. To some they do: to a person of religious, especially Christian faith, or of classical theological orientation, the texts and themes are located at the very core of spirituality. They speak to God and about God, in the motifs and languages of prayers and scripture that have endured over centuries if not millennia. But Judeo-Christian sacred texts simply do not strike a chord with everyone's personal and corporate sense of the transcendent. From a perspective of a secular spirituality, as well as from some other religious sensibilities, supplicatory prayers to the Virgin Mary or to another saint in Latin, or meditations calling attention to one's wretched sinfulness, are uncomfortable. They may even feel contrary to that which is genuine, spontaneous, essential.

Pärt's deployment of Christian source material can be made more digestible to the non-Christian by understanding it contextually: classical biblical or liturgical texts (e.g., *Missa Sylabica, Berliner Messe, Passio, Miserere, Te Deum, Nunc Dimittis*) may

---

[57]Robert Sholl, "Pärt and Spirituality," in Andrew Shenton, ed., *The Cambridge Companion to Arvo Pärt* (Cambridge: Cambridge University Press, 2012), 140–158, makes a passing mention. Hillier takes the matter much more seriously.

[58]On which, see above, at pp. 25–30.

be seen in terms of thematic reference to the history of Western music, which for centuries drew on those same passages and rites. Secular-spiritual audiences may likewise forgive Pärt for his reliance on the "religious" sources because evidently these texts have not prevented his music from being so spiritually evocative. They may even have contributed in a mysterious way to its transcendence.[59]

As I keep stressing, the music is spiritually evocative to religious and non-religious alike. Pärt's music strikes many people right to their core, moves them like an ocean; it bespeaks purity, strikes all the chords of "bright sadness"—all in ways that do not necessarily, at first blush, rely upon the texts that undergird it. Countless listeners, without ever consulting texts and/or translations, say that they are seized by the music itself, drawn out of themselves. They feel heard and consoled for their pain, stilled in their inner selves, taken to the contemplation of greater realities.[60]

So, what *is* the relationship between the text and the music? Would Pärt's music be the same with a completely different textual foundation? What would it be like had it been composed to a love sonnet?[61] Or to meditations on natural beauty, and our longing

---

[59] "Although I am not myself a 'believer', I seem to be partial to religious music, I suspect because it asks, though it cannot answer, those eternally Unanswered Questions." Mellers, *Celestial Music? Some Masterpieces of European Religious Music*, xi. Wilfrid Mellers has written at length about Pärt, including several essays that featured in his CD liner notes.

[60] An indicative comment on the Arvo Pärt Project Facebook page: "In all honesty, [the text] is irrelevant to my experience with Pärt's music. I know it is part of his process and important to him. I am not a religious person. I have always said though, that if there is anything that could possibly make me so, it would be Pärt's music."

[61] There is one example: *Es Sang vor Langen Jahren* (1984).

to be connected with it? We have hints of this last, in *My Heart's in the Highlands* (2000), which some listeners may experience as the most spiritual of all Pärt's texts, as it is the least "churchy."[62] Apart from a sharply limited set of examples, the repertoire itself gives us little to go on: it *is* set to sacred text.

That said, we must visit the crucial exceptions to the rule, those few *tintinnabuli* pieces that have no clear basis in a text. Dating from the first two years of his *tintinnabuli* repertoire, they constitute a numerically tiny portion of Pärt's post-1976 work but are among his most celebrated and enduring compositions. *Für Alina, Spiegel im Spiegel, Cantus in Memory of Benjamin Britten, Fratres,* and *Tabula Rasa,* are all iconic pieces that stand as an irrefutable reminder that, however central text is to his compositional process, he also has worked independently of text to produce works that are broadly and deeply admired, for their spirituality among other qualities.[63] These works emanate from 1976–1978, before words grew into their dominance in his compositional process.[64] But this demonstrates that the same Pärt who makes music by "clothing the text" at one point also made music without it, guided melodically, harmonically, and rhythmically by the same kinds of rules, formulas, and structural foundations he used for texted works. What we will be seeing shortly, however, is that when there *is* a text, whether audible or not, it is

---

[62]See also the lesser-known *Sei gelobt, du Baum* (2007), a hymn to a tree.

[63]See Rick Moody, as cited above at p. 37, and Arthur Lubow, who notes that "even the instrumental works bear a whiff of church incense," also cited above (p. 32).

[64]All of the works just named were composed between 1976–78. There are other textless pieces after 1978, such as *Silhouette* (2009), but these remain a very rare exception.

of fundamental importance to the piece's genesis, execution, and its very being. Before we come to that, let us reflect the relationship between word and music—a relationship with deep roots, and varied expressions.

Text and Music in History

To many ancient philosophers music and word were inextricably related. If anything, the music was subservient to the text; it required words in order to be properly received. In a sense, music did have its own power. Pythagoras was alleged to have held that the music we create taps into the "music of the spheres"—the music produced by and through the cosmos itself. The mathematical formulas and physically demonstrable proportions that guide music are the same ones that govern the universe and its planets. Taking up this reasoning, Plato insisted that music—embedded with that cosmic pedigree—is more than just pleasing: to the philosopher it could yield insight into the world's mysteries. But if people were properly to be taught by music, rather than simply be carried away with its visceral effects, they needed the words.[65] Only words could reliably guide the composition of the music; the music must follow their shape and rhythm.[66]

Plato's skepticism about text-less music extends centuries forward into early Christian sensibility. Augustine was not immune to the sheerly sensual beauty of music-as-such; he even agreed with Plato about music's "hidden affinity" with the human spirit. But human susceptibility to music made him all the more insistent

---

[65] A helpful, concise summary of Plato on this subject can be found in Begbie, *Resounding Truth: Christian Wisdom in the World of Music*, 80–82.

[66] See Plato, *Republic* 3.398d.

on text—on the words that would shepherd the listener's reaction and response. Through its potentially deceptive effect on the senses, music needed the guidance, specifically of sacred text. For its part, the text subsequently would gain greater access into the listener's heart.[67] Music and word thus belong in symbiotic relationship.

In present-day religious thought and practice we find this ancient symbiosis-in-tension alive and well. On the one hand, music is still widely seen as uniquely able to affect people specifically at the spiritual level, deeply and often unconsciously. The composer James MacMillan cites two contemporary churchmen to underscore this point:

> The Scottish Jesuit John McDade has written: "Music may be the closest human analogue to the mystery of the direct and effective communication of grace." This suggests that music is a phenomenon connected to the work of God in the way it touches something deep in our souls and releases a divine force.
>
> The Archbishop of Canterbury, Rowan Williams, in a sermon some years ago for the Three Choirs Festival, said: "To listen seriously to music and to perform it are among our most potent ways of learning what it is to live with and before God . . ."[68]

---

[67]"I feel that when the sacred words are chanted well, our souls are moved and are more religiously and with a warmer devotion kindled to piety than if they are not so sung." *Confessions* 10.33.50, cited in Begbie, op. cit., 320f, n. 36.

[68]James MacMillan, "Divine Accompaniment," *The Guardian*, July 18 2003.

These call to mind Aldous Huxley's words about the particular expressive power of music: "After silence, that which comes nearest to expressing the inexpressible is music."[69] Music is powerful, and uniquely capable of speaking the ineffable, all on its own.[70]

On the other hand there is a lingering sensibility in some circles that music requires text in order more surely to convey meaning. In the Orthodox Church of recent centuries and today, the role of untexted music is a matter of impassioned debate. There is a tradition of melismatic singing, sometimes even featuring nonsense syllables (*kratema*) that extend the melodic life of a hymn—something that would indicate the inherent value of the music itself, taking flight from its dependence upon text.[71] Recent scholarship has drawn attention to the total "soundscape" of Orthodox

[69]"The Rest Is Silence," in *Music at Night and Other Essays* (Leipzig, 1931), 19.

[70]Confidence in the power of music apart from text is reflected outside traditionally "sacred" music. The contemporary bands cited earlier (at pp. 38f.) place little emphasis on text. Our only glimpses of the music's intended meaning, outside the music itself, rests with the often cryptic or inconsequential titles (e.g., Stars of the Lid ". . . And their Refinement of the Decline," "The Evil That Never Came," "Articulate Silences," Sigur Rós "Untitled," et al. Other Pärt-loving bands such as Radiohead and REM do feature lyrics, but rarely with the pretense to profundity: Michael Stipe of REM for years sang in a deliberately unintelligible way (see Robert Sloane, "Tensions between Popular and Alternative Music: R.E.M. As an Artist-Intellectual," in *A Companion to Media Studies*, ed. Angharad N. Valdivia (Oxford: Blackwell, 2003).)—the text was not the point. The human voice is powerful, and can either murmur the words, like Stipe, or vocalize on syllables, like Jónsi Birgisson of Sigur Ros (who invented the nonsense-syllable language "Hopelandic"), but music is fully capable of delivering its goods apart from words.

[71]Alexander Lingas has directed my attention to: Gregorios Anastasiou, *Τὰ κρατήματα στὴν ψαλτικὴ τέχνη*, Institute of Byzantine Musicology Studies 12, ed. Gregorios Stathis (Athens: Institute of Byzantine Musicology, 2005).

liturgy, suggesting a role to the music that extends beyond its role as mere vehicle for text.[72] There is a still more fierce debate, academic and popular, as to whether there should be any musical instruments in church apart from the human voice.[73] Whatever one's position in these conversations, it is clear that the function of music in the Orthodox liturgy cannot be identified solely with the communication of text: the music speaks too. Yet at the risk of comparing uncomparables, there is an indisputable primacy to the text's role. It is the texts, more than the music, which claim patristic provenance and authority; it is the texts that must be vetted for their theological content. Moreover it is possible, though not ideal, to recite a liturgical office without music—as is in fact done periodically out of necessity—but it is inconceivable to serve a liturgy with music alone.

It remains best to consider music and text symbiotically. In the Orthodox Church's corporate prayer life, music constitutes an indispensable part of the experience of liturgy. It functions also in

---

[72]Alexander Lingas, "Preliminary Reflections on Studying the Liturgical Place of Byzantine and Slavonic Melismatic Chant," in *Paleobyzantine Notations III: Acta of the Congress Held at Hernen Castle, the Netherlands, in March 2001*, ed. Gerda Wolfram, Eastern Christian Studies (Leuven, Paris, and Dudley, MA: Peeters, 2004); "From Earth to Heaven: The Changing Soundscape of Byzantine Liturgy," in *Experiencing Byzantium: Papers from the 44th Spring Symposium of Byzantine Studies, Newcastle and Durham, April 2011*, ed. Claire Nesbitt and Mark Jackson, Society for the Promotion of Byzantine Studies Publications (Aldershot: Ashgate, 2013).

[73]James McKinnon summarizes the views of several early Christian authors such as Tertullian and John Chrysostom, leery of instrumental music and partial to *a capella* singing. James McKinnon, ed. *Music in Early Christian Literature* (Cambridge, UK: Cambridge University Press, 1987), 1–4. Others have contested that the ancient proscriptions applied only to their proper context and do not bear relevance to the present day.

the communication of text, either to enhance its reception through repeated musical phrases, or in some cases to give direct musical expression (through rhythm, cadence, tonality) to the prayer.

It would be easy to agree that music, generally speaking, has a profound affective power on its own, for reasons that can be boiled down to mathematics and neurology, not to mention how we all know it makes us feel. That power is potentially expressive: music is capable of conveying emotions, sensibilities, social commentaries, and *meaning*, all apart from words. Naturally, that capability is limited, usually subjective, and shaped by cultural context. The great overarching hermeneutic problem—there is no perfectly reliable communication of meaning in this world—carries its own implications for music: how can we know what a given piece of music "means to" convey? And does it even matter?[74] Setting music to a text is certainly one way of helping to identify a composition's message: the text is (broadly speaking) what the music is "about." A love poem, a prayer for mercy, an elegy, a manifesto. Whether or not the text restricts a listener's interpretation or reaction to the music, it will tell of the composition's underlying sense.

Case studies

We have not solved decisively, nor can we ever, the question of the role of the text in the listener's reception of music. There are too many variables, both at the compositional end (how intentionally does the composer relate his/her music to a given text?) and at the listener's end (how much will the listener consult or even comprehend the text of a given composition?). One can finally

---

[74]I discussed the matter of authorial intent in the introductory material, and will revisit the topic at the close of this section.

only provide some illustrations that may show tendencies. In that spirit, then, here are some examples of listeners who at first did not follow a composition's text, and then did, and what happened.

The first example belongs to Arnold Schönberg, who cites a somewhat idealized instance of how music and text *ought* to be related. Listening to some Schubert lieder, he realized that he had never actually paid attention to what their poetic texts were saying. He feared that he must have been missing what the music was "about." So, what happened when he actually read the poems? "It became clear to me that I had gained absolutely nothing for the understanding of the songs." Why was that? Because the music bore no relation to the text? "On the contrary, it appeared that, without knowing the poem, I had grasped [its] content, the real content, perhaps even more profoundly than if I had clung to the surface of the [. . .] words."[75] He goes on to describe his own experience with setting text to music, where he was able to grasp and, in a kind of intuitive "ecstasy," convey the spirit of the text musically. For Schönberg, then, text and music ought to be so thoroughly integrated as to be transparent to each other. Or better still, so that the music can evoke the words' innate and invisible force, through a deep and instinctive fusion—or perhaps both conspire to express a common poetic idea. The result for Schönberg, in any event, is that just as the DNA of an entire organism is found in each cell of that organism, so the "sense" of the text must flow from the entirety of the music, or from any part of it.[76]

[75]Arnold Schoenberg, "The Relationship to the Text," in *Style and Idea: Selected Writings of Arnold Schoenberg*, ed. Leonard Stein (Berkeley, CA: University of California Press, 1984 [1912]), 144.

[76]Schönberg's somewhat more gruesome metaphor here is blood—the same exact blood courses through an organism's veins, so that when you cut into any part of its body, the same thing comes out. (Ibid.)

Schönberg's example calls to mind a story from the desert fathers. A disciple, who would typically ask a monastic father or mother "a word." The "word" would be a saying or a teaching, short or long. But one monk used to visit Abba Anthony regularly, without ever asking for a "word." Why? Because "It is enough for me to see you."[77] The word is so embedded in the person that it need not even be expressed.

My second example shows that the word, the text, can make a significant difference in the appropriation of a piece of music. It consists in the reactions reported to me by experienced Pärt listeners at a recent concert. I co-produced a performance of *Adam's Lament* on May 31, 2014, at Carnegie Hall. At Arvo and Nora Pärt's suggestion, we arranged for the text to be projected in English translation on the wall behind the musicians, synchronized with the performance. Limor Tomer, curator of music and lectures at the Metropolitan Museum of Art, had the following reaction: "That was a mean trick!" she chided me, only half-jokingly. What did she mean by that? "You devastated all of us!" she continued, "You projected that text, and because it was set to this amazing music, we could let it in—we were defenseless." As Tomer says,

> It cuts through all the cynicism, the "meta" of the twenty-first-century listener, for whom every interaction has to be mediated. That existential dread, the feeling of being a wretch—that feeling is actually at the core of the postmodern noise, and coming face to face with it, without a place to hide—this was unspeakably powerful.[78]

---

[77]Ibid., 6.
[78]Phone conversation with Limor Tomer, July 10, 2014.

Apart from her perceptive commentary on the text of *Adam's Lament* in contemporary context, what are we to take from Tomer's comments? Schönberg's experience of Schubert's music was unchanged by his discovery of its text. She found the experience of text-with-music transformative. There may be several reasons for this, apart from the significant differences between composers, texts, listeners, and eras. The effect that Schönberg describes is generalized: it pertains to the broad, collective ethos of both the text and the music. Schönberg does not mention the quality or character of the poem, or whether he even liked it. The effect on Tomer has primarily to do with the text, which could more easily insinuate itself into her consciousness on the wings of the music. And the music was a fitting vehicle, a translation, as it were, of the text: "It was knowing what the singers were singing; seeing them utter the words, sometimes literally through tears in their eyes; and experiencing viscerally the words becoming corporeal, taking on volume, through the sound."[79]

The same piece, performed with supertitles at the "White Lights" festival at Lincoln Center on November 17, 2012, engendered the following reaction from composer and music educator Nicholas Reeves:

> Since the written meditation "Adam's Lament" is the driving force behind Pärt's composition, both the narrative and the contours of the (text-driven) musical composition were made clear in content and emotion by the supertitles. With the titles as a focal point, I was brought to a content-oriented listening as opposed to a orchestral-oriented listening. My mind, initially drawn to the text projected on a screen, soon

[79]Ibid.

68

sunk into my heart as the dramatic interpretation of the text was amplified by the choir and string orchestra. I have certainly been moved by instrumental music on its own merits, but the emotional experience I had at the White Lights festival was made possible by the encounter of the music with its words. I was brought to an experience of the latent power of both.[80]

A further factor here lies with the programmatic nature of the composition. *Adam's Lament* is a musical journey through multiple textures and tonalities, with a wide dynamic and sonic range. When the narrator describes Adam's fall, the music turns sour. When he enumerates the suffering of humanity to come, the music becomes cataclysmic. When he begs God for a spirit of love and mercy, the music turns tender. It is, effectively, program music, and will naturally be better understood when the text and the music come into alignment with each other.

At the root of these diverse experiences lies the basic fact that text plays an indisputable (if varied) role, at both ends of a composition's life: in its composition and in its reception. Some compositions more than others have a memorable text right at the forefront of the listening experience.[81] Some more than others are received in a new and deeper way through familiarity with the text.[82] Thus far we have focused only on the effect the text has on the listener. As for the composer, we may say that, whatever its role, the text represents a deliberate choice that will affect the composition to a greater or lesser extent. As we are about to see,

---

[80]Unpublished conversation with Nicholas Reeves, September 8, 2014.
[81]*The Deer's Cry,* for example, has this effect, on English speakers.
[82]As we saw was the case for many listeners of *Adam's Lament.*

once he began to use text in his music, its role became clear: it is fundamental, essential, primary.

Pärt and Text: In the Beginning

The words write my music.

Arvo Pärt

"In the beginning was the Word." Thus reads the striking first phrase of the Gospel of John.[83] This and the next 17 verses constitute what is known as the "Johannine Prologue," a significant text in the history of ideas generally, and in Christian theology in specific. Some of its basic concepts are worth exploring. "Word" here is a weak rendering of the Greek "Logos," whose entry in ancient and patristic Greek lexicons runs for several pages. Its meaning is multifaceted, its roots long. Pre-Christian Stoic philosophy saw the Logos as "the world's soul," its underlying principle, its inner reason or logic.[84] But the Stoics did not connect the Logos with an eternal, personal God. John's Gospel and subsequent Christian theology adopted and reshaped the Stoics' idea, telling us that the Logos/Word, is eternal—specifically, *co*-eternal with God. The God known as the God of Abraham, Isaac, and Jacob, has a "Word," a self-expression. If we can imagine a single word perfectly presenting our total self, this is how ancient Christians understood the Logos: God's unique and complete self-expression. God's Word, known also as God's "Son," is co-essential with God, it/he is divine as God is.[85] It is furthermore a *creative* Word—the whole world comes into being through it.[86]

[83] John 1:1. All biblical translations are taken from the Revised Standard Version.

[84] We may take note of the etymology of the word "logic."

[85] We are still at John 1:1.

[86] John 1:3.

So that before we even get to the identity of that Word—Jesus Christ[87]—we see that Word/Logos/*verbum* carries a far-reaching set of meanings and implications—again, in philosophy generally, and in Christian theology in specific. The root concepts of rationality, essential principle, logic, are all lodged and sourced within the Logos/Word.

"In the beginning was the Word"—in Latin, *In Principio erat verbum*. That phrase, and all that underlies it, looms large in Pärt's self-understanding as a composer. His 2003 composition *In Principio* is a setting of the Johannine Prologue. *In Principio* is also the title of the first book published by the Arvo Pärt Centre; it is a complete collection of the texts that the composer has set to music. Pärt is deeply invested in John's concept of Word/Logos/*Verbum*. Words are important to him not only because they underlie and dictate the shape of his melodies, nor only because of their power to communicate meaning. They are properly rooted in the divine Word himself, and as such are *sacred*. If anyone is to plumb the role of text in Pärt's post-1976 compositions, they must inevitably do so from theological depth of the concept of "word/Word." As he puts it,

> These mystic words of the Gospel according to John, "In the beginning was the Word," lie at the heart of it all, since without the Word, nothing would exist. I believe that this concept should not only be conveyed in the text, but in every note of the music as well, in every thought, in every stone. The roots of our skill lie in this thought: "In the beginning was the Word."[88]

[87]John 1:14.
[88]Restagno, 66.

Elsewhere, he notes, "Sound is my word. I am convinced that sound should also speak of what the Word determines. The Word, which was in the beginning."[89]

At the very outset of his book on Pärt, Paul Hillier describes Pärt's approach to words against the relief of other composers'. One kind of composer, Hillier observes, " 'sets' a religious text, but uses a style which is essentially unaltered by the nature of the words and their theological or liturgical context." But there is another type—and here he is obviously describing Pärt—"for whom these [sacred/liturgical] texts are the very breath of life, and who probably cannot imagine himself working with any other kind."[90]

Pärt has made his own characteristically succinct, pithy statements about the fundamental role of text in his process of composition. "The words write my music."[91] He has spoken of his music as merely "translations of the text." It is as if the words still do the talking, only in another "language," namely, that of music. Another, not dissimilar way of putting it is that the texts contain within themselves a latent music. "The texts [. . .] possess their own music, which must merely be brought forth."[92]

---

[89]Epigraph to Kristina Kõrver et al., *In Principio*.

[90]Hillier, *Arvo Pärt*, x.

[91]See Toomas Siitan's introduction to *In Principio*, op. cit., 13. Pärt refers to this oft-cited quote in Geoff Smith, "Sources of Invention: An Interview with Arvo Pärt," *The Musical Times*, 140 (Autumn 1999), 19–25.: "My claim to let words write their own music makes some people laugh, particularly music journalists."

[92]Toomas Siitan, in *In Principio*, op. cit. 11.

Means of Textual Engagement

The primal role of the text in the generation of Pärt's composi-tions is sometimes more and sometimes less discernable. That role will always encompass two interwoven elements:

- The ways in which words, their syllables, their stress, and the punctuation that separates them, will dictate the shape and rhythm of the melody. We will call these the "syllabic rules."

- How the piece manages to evoke or "translate" the *sense* of the words through the language of music.

Hillier summarizes these parallel processes: Pärt's approach "works outwards from the structure of the text and, simultane-ously, inwards from the significance of the text as a whole (his-torically, spiritually, and liturgically)."[93] The processes are indeed parallel, simultaneous. The syllabic rules can make a text more comprehensible, especially if one knows the language of the text (Latin, Slavonic, English, etc.). But it is more than that: there seems to be a conviction that the words, the syllables themselves, bear a potency such that if the composer heeds their rhythm in their respective language, he is conveying their sense in any language.

For *Adam's Lament,* Pärt comments, "I wanted to remain as close as possible to Silouan's words and, as far as I could, to entrust myself with them, to internalize them."[94] He is speaking here to the goal of overall translation of Silouan's text, even as this is among his works that are composed according to syllable-driven rules.

---

[93]Hillier, *Arvo Pärt*, x.
[94]William Robin, "His Music, Entwined with His Faith," *The New York Times*, May 16, 2014 2014.

Rules

Let us now say more about the syllabic formulae. Such rules have a long history that dates back at least to plainchant as well as the synagogue practice of cantillation—the ritual chanting of the Hebrew Bible. Plato, as we will recall, said that music ought to follow the rhythms of words.[95] These principles are intended to enhance the articulation and hence the comprehension of the texts being sung—a practice with roots that go deep into the history of music. Taking his cues from this history, and in particular as it applied to settings of the Passion of Christ,[96] Pärt's *Passio* is among his clearest and most sustained applications of rigorously applied formulas, that I will here summarize briefly.[97]

As the text of St John's passion[98] is sung, the notes can have any of three different durations: long, medium, and short. The note is *long* in all syllables of a word that ends a sentence or clause.[99] The note is *medium* in the syllable preceding a comma, in the first stressed syllable in a new sentence, and in all the syllables of a word preceding a question mark. All other syllables are *short*. These are relative values, which change depending on who is speaking: the values are shortest during the Evangelist's narration, and longest during the words of Christ.

The *Passio* is governed by other formulas as well; for example—again following centuries-old precedent—each "character" (Jesus,

---

[95]See Plato, *Republic* 3.398d.

[96]See Kurt von Fischer, "Passion," in *The New Grove Dictionary of Music and Musicians*, ed. Stanley Sadie (London: Macmillan, 1980), 277.

[97]The complete title of the work, composed in 1982, is *Passio Domini Nostri Jesu Christi secundum Joannem*. The rules I summarize here are set out more completely in Hillier, *Arvo Pärt*, 127f.

[98]John 18:1–19:30.

[99]I.e, a word followed by a period/full-stop, or a colon.

Pilate, the Evangelist-narrator, and the crowd or *Turba*) has its own tonality and register, its own voice. But Pärt's genius lies in his creation and deployment of these rules. They are not immediately apparent to the listener's conscious mind: they work subliminally to evoke a powerful dramatization amid what may seem to be an emotionally neutral, "formulaic" project. Again, structure, formula, rule—these do not merely receive living expression in the piece, they somehow *give* the piece its life. In this way, the text reigns; the music has fulfilled its role as the text's vehicle, an evocation of the text's inherent music. Pärt's perception of his role as mere translator, his statement that "The words write my music"—these are meant to evoke the goal of the music's transparency to its text. But they deceptively downplay the composer's part: he is effectively bringing words into a language that he himself has created, and which is capable of being understood by the speakers of any tongue. As at Pentecost.[100]

Silent Text

The evocation of text in Pärt's work can take mysterious turns. The same kind of rules, based on syllables and punctuation, are at the basis of numerous compositions where we do not even hear the text, where the listener is in most cases completely unaware of the text's existence.[101] A listing of such compositions follows, together with their underlying text. (There are also a few works originally set to texts and then re-set in instrumental orchestrations.)[102]

[100]Acts 2:1–12. The Pentecost event features people of diverse nations and tongues, inspired by the Holy Spirit, speaking a single language that is understood universally.

[101]Interestingly, nearly all the "silent" texts behind these compositions are in Slavonic or Russian.

[102]*Solfeggio, Summa, In Spe/An den Wassern zu Babel, Da pacem Domine, Missa Brevis,* and *Swansong/Littlemore Tractus.*

- *Psalom* (1985)—Psalm 112 (113), in Slavonic.
- *Silouan's Song* (1991)—Excerpt from St Silouan's "Adam's Lament," in Russian.
- *Trisagion* (1992)—Introductory prayers in Slavonic.
- *Orient & Occident* (2000)—The Nicene Creed, in Slavonic.
- *Lamentate* (2002)—Troparia of repentance in Slavonic, with verses from *Dies Irae* in Latin.
- *Für Lennart In Memoriam* (2006)—Irmos 6 from the Canon of Repentance (also sung at funeral and memorial services), and a prayer by Archimandrite Sophrony (Sakharov), both in Slavonic.
- Symphony No. 4 "Los Angeles" (2008)[103]—Canon to the Guardian Angel, in Slavonic.

The role of the text in these cases is on the one hand clear-cut: when it comes to compositional process, the text functions in an identical fashion as with those pieces where the text is actually heard, with often a direct relationship between the music and the text's syllables, stresses, and punctuation, as we saw above in *Passio*. Yet we may ask: to what degree is the composition really conveying, or even translating its silent underlying text? Answers to that question—again by nature subjective—will vary depending on the composition in question, and on the listener. To illustrate, three more case studies, from my own background.

Für Lennart, written in memory of Estonian statesman and artist Lennart Meri,[104] powerfully and clearly evokes the Slavonic

---

[103]Symphony No. 4 also includes portions of the composition *These Words*, from the same year.

[104]Meri was an Estonian Renaissance man: writer, film director, leader

funeral hymns that dictate its rhythm. Here, my own reaction mirrors that of Schönberg to Schubert's *Lieder*. I listened to this piece for years unaware of its textual origins. Once I learned of its basis in the Orthodox funeral hymns I found that I gained little or no insight into the piece, for it had already conveyed the meaning and feeling of those hymns perfectly. The text and music are a complete unison, both a balance of sorrow and hope.

I experienced a completely different reaction with *Orient/Occident,* a piece which (as I only later learned) had been composed to the words of the Nicene Creed. It is a beautiful and striking work, stylistically unlike anything Pärt had composed before. But its connection to the *meaning* of the Nicene Creed escapes me. The piece conveys a sense of urgency and focus, which one might, I suppose, take as an indication of how seriously the composer takes the foundations of Christian faith enumerated in the Creed. It is not as if he could have written the same work based on a page from a telephone directory, yet neither does the connection with the Creed feel inevitable. If this piece feels especially disconnected from the text, it may owe partly to its basis in an additional rule not found elsewhere in Pärt's corpus: with each word of the Slavonic text it oscillates between two sharply contrasting tonalities—Oriental and Occidental respectively. (The first word, "Верую" ["I-believe"], is voiced in the "Occidental" tonality.) Are we being shown that the Nicene Creed is an ecumenical text, spanning East and West in its influence? It is neither an unlikely nor an inexorable conclusion. But it is hard to see the music as having "translated" this theologically rich text.

of the Estonian independence movement, and the republic's president from 1992 to 2001.

Squarely in between these two experiences for me was *Trisagion*. Here too, I had not known of its textual basis in the classic Orthodox introductory prayers in Slavonic. Now that I do know, it seems obvious, and it has completely transformed my experience of the work. As music, this piece—however attractive—had never made a great deal of sense to me, but now I cannot listen to it without silently reciting these prayers, which I know by heart. The prayers and the music now come alive together, as they before had not.

Again, these matters are affective and therefore subjective in their character. But the examples above illustrate a range of possibilities in the collective experience of text and music.

The Choice of Language

As is becoming increasingly obvious through this narrative, the syllabic rules do not pre-program the music's ethos, nor do they determine a lock-step adherence to the text's purported meaning. This is made clear in another phenomenon commonly observed in Pärt's work: even when the words "form" the music through the formulae, the resulting compositions are liable to sound completely different. One significant factor is the composer's choice of language. Pärt has set his music to texts in English, German, Latin, Estonian, Spanish, Italian, French, Russian, and Church Slavonic. Is it an entirely subjective observation that many of Pärt's compositions set to Latin texts (e.g., *Salve Regina, Stabat Mater*) sound "Western European," whereas texts in Slavic languages, (*Adam's Lament, Silouan's Song, Kanon Pokajanen*) sound Russian?

In any communication, the choice of language will be significant. A language's given structure and syntax, even its sound, will have a bearing on the substance of what is expressed and heard.[105] In the case of music, the decision to set a composition to a text in Latin, Slavonic, German, or Italian can also entail a commitment to that language's particular musical legacy. Slavic sensibilities, intertwined with church sensibilities, informed the Russian musical world for centuries, such that a contemporary composition to a Slavonic text will often take that history on board, effectively perpetuating it even while introducing something new.[106]

Pärt himself notices something like this in the case of the *Kanon*:

> In this composition, as in many of my vocal works, I tried to use language as a point of departure. I wanted the word to be able to find its own sound, to draw its own melodic line. Somewhat to my surprise, the resulting music is entirely immersed in the particular character of Church Slavonic [. . .].[107]

He continues,

> The *Kanon* has shown me how much the choice of language predetermines the character of a work, so much so, in fact, that the entire structure of the musical composition

---

[105]Philosophers have noted, for example, that languages where the modifier precedes the subject (speaking, e.g., of "a red apple") will have a different concept of reality than those where the modifier follows it ("une pomme rouge"). We are talking about nominalism vs realism.

[106]This may explain why some listeners detect the influence of Russian church music in Pärt's work.

[107]CD liner notes, *Kanon Pokajanen* (ECM 1654/55, 1998).

is subject to the text and its laws: one lets the language "create the music." The same musical structure, the same treatment of the word, leads to different results depending on the choice of language, as seen on comparing *Litany* (English) with *Kanon Pokajanen* (Church Slavonic). I used identical, strictly defined rules of composition and yet the outcome is very different in each case.[108]

The effect of language choice varies among Pärt's compositions; sometimes it is greater (such as in the examples I listed above), sometimes less. *Triodion* (1998) is an interesting case: the text is in English, drawn from a Russian Orthodox prayer setting, set to music whose character alternates between Eastern and Western European tonalities.[109]

* * *

In these pages we have not drawn many binding and universal conclusions about the relationship between text and music. We did establish that there were two bookends to that relationship, namely the role of the text for the composer and the compositional process, and the role of the text for the listener. The ultimately unbridgeable gap between artist and audience, between author and reader, is a well-known problem I have alluded to earlier on. I would only suggest that since you, the reader, are seeking to come closer to Pärt's world, an attention to his texts may provide some significant, transformative access.

It could be argued, to the contrary, that the listener need not consult the text at all: it is enough only that the composer was

[108]Ibid. Insights on this idea may be found in Paul Ricoeur, *On Translation*, trans. Eileen Brennan (London & New York: Routledge, 2006), 15–16.

[109]I am grateful to Paul Hillier for pointing this out to me.

moved by the text and found such spiritual richness in it. If the texts of the Latin Mass, or the Beatitudes, or of St Silouan's writings, find their way into Arvo Pärt's spiritual core, and if he is uniquely capable of rendering his personal stirrings into music, it is sufficient. The textual origins were important at the point of origin, but not at the point of delivery; the spiritual content has been conveyed, translated. And just as when we read *The Canterbury Tales* in translation, and leave it to the experts to consult the original Middle English, so it is that we listen to Pärt's music.

The viability of such an approach is testified to by all those who are spiritually moved by Pärt's work without following their textual foundations. Yet that does not mean that the "spiritual delivery" is comprehensive—the *Canterbury Tales* metaphor is imperfect. In the end, a transformative appreciation of Pärt's work is not completely dependent upon consulting the text, but I would submit that it is deepened. It is enriched, and not only for an understanding of the music's rhythmic foundations but for a sense of its inner life. And this is especially so when we reflect on the texts' content and meaning.

The Text's Content

We have so far spoken about the text's role in (sometimes literally) shaping Pärt's music. Through the forms and sounds of the words, and through their meaning—both overall and phrase-by-phrase, the words constitute the skeletal structure on which his music is hung and which gives it its form. I have alluded as well to how seriously Pärt takes the concept of words and their connection to the eternal Word of God heralded at the beginning of John's gospel. That all led me to suggest that those who wish to know his music more intimately do well to examine its underlying texts, to find the words' shape, consider their language, and their context.

There is another reason to pay particular attention to the texts Pärt chooses: he actually believes in what they are saying. He sees them as sacred. They are neither cultural relics, nor fossils of a lost, venerable spiritual tradition. They are for him timeless words of life. This entails that, apart from considering their shape, language, and context, listeners may want to consider their *meaning*. This need not entail conversion or a change in spiritual orientation. It is only a natural step in taking his music seriously, given who he is and how he writes.

The consideration of Pärt's texts will lead religious believers and non-believers, people who pray and people who don't, on different journeys. The composer himself is emphatic that the appreciation of his music does not *require* convergence with his beliefs. His expectations of that convergence are humble and realistic: "It is possible that people who follow my music with interest [. . .] are like me, are in search of something and when listening to my music feel that it is moving in the same direction as they are."[110] That said, and with no expectation of perfect union between composer and listener, it would still seem that the appreciation of his music is enriched by an increased awareness of what is important to him, and what his texts mean to him.

Countless composers through history have employed biblical and liturgical texts. For some, these have a kind of inherent beauty, hearkening nostalgically to a once-held faith.[111] For others, they

---

[110]Restagno, 57f.

[111]This is likely the case for Rachmaninoff, who wrote his *All-Night Vigil*

are beautiful poetry. However valid these motivations, they are different than those of a composer who prays the texts' content and considers them to be sacred.

> I have always allowed myself to be guided by texts that mean a lot to me and that for me are of existential significance. It is a root that reaches very deep and that lifts me upwards.

Pärt then says that we have to "meet" these texts, which are timeless in their significance to humanity. "This meeting happens when the texts are not treated as literature or works of art but as points of reference, or as models." He goes on:

> The Psalms of David are also poetry, but they are not just poetry. They are part of the Holy Scripture. [. . .]They are bound to universal truths, so do they touch upon intimate truths, purity, beauty, that ideal core to which each human being is bound![112]

In pointing to the inner beauty and timeless relevance of the Scriptural texts, he suggests that this beauty is dependent upon a "meeting," an engaged encounter with them where we are vulnerable to their word. As we have seen, Pärt is not doctrinaire about his faith, nor does he wear the badge of Orthodoxy on his sleeve. Yet we have also seen that he believes deeply in what is being proclaimed in the scriptural, liturgical, and ascetical texts that he chooses.

---

to the texts of liturgical services that he no longer attended, in a Church he no longer believed in, but that resonated deeply with his personal and national history. The exact significance and meaning of "the sacred," and of the Orthodox Church specifically, to post-imperial Russian artists and writers, in and outside Russia, is a broad and ultimately inscrutable subject.

[112]Restagno, 55.

That being the case, all that we have been observing about the role of the word (and the Word) in Pärt's process suggests that the texts hold an important key to that journey. They will bring us closer to his music, partly because they mean so inestimably much to him as he is shaping it. After all, why would he create rules where the words, syllables, and punctuation guide the music's shape, other than to make the words *sing*, so that they might be comprehended and received? By opening ourselves to the words that are so important to him, we are helping to effect that meeting he speaks of, so that the trains, out of whose windows we are peering, might be more synchronized in their direction and speed. This way, we just might be afforded more than a fleeting glance at each other.

As this book's journey continues to unfold, we will begin to see how these underlying principles, the concepts lodged within the texts, find their way into musical expression. This will be important for us to uncover, because however primary the text is—"In the *beginning* was the w/Word"—his world is that of music. Arvo Pärt is not a missionary or preacher, he is a composer. He works with sound, with music; these constitute his métier. But the "he" who works with sound and music is also a person of Christian faith, who professes to be shaped by the words and rites of that faith.

II: Out of Silence

Before you can be resurrected, you must die.
Before you say something, perhaps you should say nothing.

Arvo Pärt[1]

In a recent interview Arvo Pärt's attention was turned to the theme of silence. Here was what came to his mind:

> On the one hand, silence is like fertile soil, which, as it were, awaits our creative act, our seed. On the other hand, silence must be approached with a feeling of awe. When we speak about silence, we must keep in mind that it has two different wings, so to speak. Silence can be both that which is outside of us and that which is inside a person. The silence of our soul, which isn't even affected by external distractions, is actually more crucial but more difficult to achieve.[2]

These reflections introduce several leitmotifs that will run throughout this section. With the metaphor "fertile soil," Pärt identifies silence with a potentiality out of which something may sprout. He distinguishes between external silence (measurable in

---

[1]Cited in Lothar Mattner, "Arvo Pärt: *Tabula Rasa*," *Music and Literature* 1, no. 1 (2012), 52.

[2]Arvo Pärt, in an interview with Tom Huizenga, in "The Silence and Awe of Arvo Pärt," NPR, June 2, 2014. http://www.npr.org/blogs/deceptivecadence/2014/06/02/316322238/the-silence-and-awe-of-arvo-prt, accessed July 1, 2014.

---

decibels) and interior silence. This latter is an internal stillness, an inner composure which must be cultivated, so that it might produce a right word, a right sound.

In the pages that follow we will explore the factors that led to Pärt's period of compositional impasse after 1968, as well as those that led him into an entirely new mode of conceiving music. We will see how his silence of crisis led gradually to a silence of poise and stillness. And finally we will plumb the Eastern Christian tradition for insights on the nature of silence with an eye to their relevance for Pärt's creative process and his work. Throughout, we will be finding that silence though technically an absence of sound, can also be understood as a presence: that it is not neutral but rather can bear any of a diverse set of characteristics.

Music Lost to Silence

The years between 1968 and 1976 are typically known as Arvo Pärt's "silent period," or his "eight-year silence." This characterization is not entirely misleading, neither is it precise. It is a crucial time of transition that begins with a kind of "death" following *Credo* (1968) and ends with the "birth" of *Für Alina* (1976). These eight years are indeed marked by a near-complete compositional impasse. The one major piece that emerged from this interstice, Symphony No. 3 (1971) was a work of transition, neither repeating the past nor yet heralding a way out of it. There were also around 20 film scores that came later on, but these were merely a way for Pärt to stay afloat.[3] Technically, then, the "eight-year

[3] *Ukuaru Waltz* was one of over twenty film scores that Pärt wrote during this period, and the only one that he would come to work up as a component of his formal repertoire (and not until 2010). Another work, *Laul*

silence" describes three-years where he was compositionally mute, then the third symphony, and then the purely utilitarian film work that served no function in his compositional odyssey.

These were years of profound ferment and change that were finally marked by their result: the birth of a completely new compositional style, a fresh way of thinking that would change the composer's life and make an indelible mark on the history of music. 1968–1976 is rightly considered a "period" for Arvo Pärt; associating it with silence is fully apt. The question justly arises: What silenced the composer?

Creative Impasse

With hindsight, it is not difficult to trace the journey to the creative cul-de-sac of 1968 through Pärt's compositions from the four years prior. On the one hand, they can be understood in terms of the musical context out of which they emerged: the 1960s Eastern European *avant garde*. This period was characterized by late expressions of serialism—the 12-tone style was showing at the same time a greater diversity of expression and experimentation (such as through "collage" techniques, splicing together music of different styles, sometimes from pre-existing compositions), as well as a kind of nihilism that reflected the dreadful strictures of life and art under Soviet regimes. By this time Pärt had proved himself a recognized, talented, and countercultural figure. He was the first Estonian composer to employ the 12-tone method, initially facing criticism and then emulation for his deployment of that system. And of course he was under erratic

---

Armastatule, dates from 1974, but Pärt considers it unfinished and has withdrawn it from his catalogue.

suspicion within the notoriously intertwined worlds of culture and Soviet politics.

Solfeggio (1963) represents perhaps the beginnings of a two-fold movement in Pärt's work: it hearkens back to traditional tonality, set amidst dissonance. The piece consists in nothing but an ascending major scale—the antithesis of abstraction and alienation. And yet its ingenious use of sustained notes, sometimes across registers, not only obscures the diatonic scale but reveals its latent tensions and resolutions. The dissonant seconds and ninths resolve into consonances and therefore into clear tonal centers—which serialism abhors. Following *Solfeggio* Pärt began employing collage techniques for several important works, pasting together often disparate styles. This entailed juxtapositions between sometimes deliberately harsh and alienating serial passages and incursions of an almost surrealistically sublime and traditional tonality, often directly quoted from Bach. This is what we hear in *Collage sur B-A-C-H* (1964), *Pro et Contra* (1966), and most especially in *Credo* (1968). With hindsight, the collage works are already testifying to a creative soul in profound turmoil, a piecemeal search for healing. As Pärt's himself puts it:

> I was like skin that got burnt and I needed a skin graft. One piece of new skin at a time. New live tissue was needed and planted on my burnt spots. They were my collages, and these pieces started to grow together after a while.[4]

These works tell of Pärt's acute perception of the emotional and compositional limitations of a modernism that, as Hillier

[4]From a 2005 interview conducted by Immo Mihkelson, cited in Mihkelson's "A Narrow Path to the Truth: Arvo Pärt and the 1960s and 1970s in Soviet Estonia," in Shenton, ed., *Cambridge Companion*, 10–28, p. 25.

suggests, he came to see as a hopeless attempt to escape reality, even beauty: "The glimpses of tonality in these earlier works are like intimations of a paradisiacal garden from which exile is felt to be increasingly futile."[5] In contrast to other composers' use of collage,[6] Pärt's quotations from Bach and Tchaikovsky[7] are never ironic, but reverential. They seem to be telling us how lovely music could sound, how beautiful it *used to* sound—maybe more beautiful, more *meaningful* than this contemporary serial material.[8] These are tonal islands amid a sea of music that, for all its meticulous and virtuosic character, speaks of estrangement. Of course, many avant garde compositions were unapologetically alienating and alienated, arising from the existentialism and nihilism of the age.[9] Pärt's was a kind of meta-estrangement, an alienation from alienating music. Modernism had come with the promise of liberty, in the form of freedom from the limitations of tonal centers and the strictures of cadence. For Pärt it rather quickly became the opposite: not only limited, but dead. The twelve-tone method, eschewing any tonal center by giving equal weight to all notes, became meaningless, even deleterious: "The sterile democracy

[5]P. 35.

[6]E.g., Shostakovich's *The Nose,* and several of Berio's works.

[7]E.g., in Symphony No. 2 (1966).

[8]Pärt's comments, in an interview from 1968, are interesting on this point: "I think the modernity of Bach's music will not vanish in another two hundred years, and perhaps never will. . . . The reason is not just that in absolute terms it could simply be better than contemporary music . . . [it is a matter of] how thoroughly has the author-composer perceived . . . in the totality of life, its joy, worries, and mysteries . . ." Cited in Paul Hillier, *Arvo Pärt,* 65.

[9]See e.g., Pierre Boulez's work, *Le Marteau Sans Maître.* The 1960s were a watershed in literary criticism as well, with, e.g., Jacques Derrida's "Structure, Sign, and Play in the Discourse of the Human Sciences," often cited as the beginning of post-structuralism, coming onto the scene in 1966.

between the notes has killed in us every living feeling."[10] Pärt says elsewhere,

> ... I was convinced that I just could not go on with the compositional means at my disposal. There simply wasn't enough material to go on with, so I just stopped composing altogether. I wanted to find something that was alive and simple and not destructive.[11]

Several composers (e.g., György Ligeti, Krzysztof Penderecki) were taking exception to serialist modernism in the 1960s, each with his own way of revolting against it. Pärt's mutiny took place through collage, which he expressed in juxtapositions between sublime harmony and utter cacophony that are particularly striking, even violent, in *Credo*. That work, significant in its own right in the history of twentieth century music, represents the climax or at least the end-point of Pärt's 1960s creative output.

Listening to *Credo* reveals a great creative mind at the very end of its tether. *Credo* is characterized by bold musical statements—there is nothing tentative throughout—but largely by the stark contrasts that it presents. Passages based on Bach's Prelude in C, sometimes intact, sometimes retrograde, are set against dense twelve-note clusters, with the choir progressing from a forceful whisper to the top of their dynamic range (the score is marked *feroce, fff*). In between there are passages, written according to strict rules and following serial tone-rows, that herald and effect the transitions between sublime, familiar, traditional harmony, and cacophonous, absurd, modernist dissonance.

---

[10]Martin Elste, "An Interview with Arvo Pärt," *Fanfare* 11, no. March/April (1988).
[11]Restagno, 27.

Credo had an explosive cultural impact—so much so that as soon as the performance was over the audience insisted that it be repeated then and there. It was the most talked-about cultural event of its day.[12] And yet, hearing it today one cannot but have the impression of witnessing, together with something bizarrely sublime, a creative and spiritual unraveling. It was the full-stop before the silence. Music history presented him with no apparent options: Bach had been done and could not be outdone, but the alternatives presented by the 1960s avant-garde were unacceptable. The piece resonates like a sustained cry: "I CAN'T DO THIS ANYMORE."

But as hindsight makes clear, *Credo* was the kind of death that would result in new life: "*Credo* was like a seed; the hidden model of a germinating organism that had to die in order for it to bear fruit."[13]

Political Censure

In addition to artistic challenges, Pärt and his colleagues suffered the extreme vicissitudes of a state whose controlling tentacles insinuated themselves deeply into the arts. Serialism itself went in and out of favor, composers had to toe the Party line musically and ideologically to different extents, if they were to remain viable. Pärt's *Nekrolog* (1960–61), Estonia's first serial composition, was sharply criticized for having adopted the "Western" 12-tone method. Yet that same year Pärt won a prestigious and exclusive Soviet composers' prize.

---

[12]Ibid.
[13]Toomas Siitan, in *In Principio*, 10. (See John 12:24.)

The sung text at the heart of *Credo* "I believe in Jesus Christ," should have prevented it from being performed, and Pärt tells of the remarkable touch-and-go circumstances that allowed it to elude the censors for its premier performance.[14] In the end, however, partly owing to the huge splash created by that event, and partly owing to the authorities' embarrassment at having let it slip past, it ended up causing the composer an increase in political harassment. Presumed (owing to its title) to be a setting of the Nicene Creed, it was taken as an outright provocation against the strictly atheist regime and was banned, from performance and even from mention, for a solid decade within the Soviet Union.[15]

Credo is a remarkable and pivotal work. Musically, as we have seen, it is a jarring amalgam. As we will see below it was also a spiritual manifesto. But it was a political statement as well: Pärt in hindsight likens aspects of its structure as representing the breakup of the Soviet regime.[16] But the piece did not cause its composer to be expelled from the Soviet Union; he left much later, in 1980. He remained in Estonia through the entirety of his silent/transition period; he also stayed through some especially challenging years of Estonia's two Soviet occupations, during which the state cultural officials treated him with "constant animosity."[17] But the political attention and increased suspicion that he drew to himself with *Credo* added significantly to that tumultuous and finally heartbreaking year of 1968 that rendered him compositionally mute.

[14]Restagno, 26.
[15]The story is recounted in Restagno, 25–26.
[16]Restagno, 27.
[17]Restagno, 44.

Spiritual Odyssey

Pärt's compositional silence was thus a creative impasse, with strong political factors. But as I have intimated it also had to do with a spiritual crisis. Let us look once again at *Credo*. Apart from everything else, it represents Pärt's first musical setting of a spiritual text. The "Credo" of the title is not the Nicene Creed that was foundational to Christian tradition, and which has been set to music by countless composers. Pärt's "Credo" is a self-standing statement, a paraphrase of an excerpt from the Creed: *Credo in Jesum Christum* ("I believe in Jesus Christ") plus wording from Matthew 5:38–39: *Audivistis dictum: oculum pro oculo, dentem pro dente. Autem ego vobis dico: non esse resistendum injuriae* ("You have heard that it was said, 'An eye for an eye and a tooth for a tooth.' But I say to you, Do not resist one who is evil"). The two concepts are at a complete moral and spiritual contrast. The vindictive logic of eye-for-eye, cited in Leviticus and Deuteronomy but associated also with the eighteenth century BCE Babylonian Code of Hammurabi, is set against Christ's own nonviolent injunction to turn the other cheek. The ethical contrasts give rise to the harmonic oscillations described above, the unforgiving morality being shouted in harsh note-clusters by the choir, and Christ's commandment set to Bach's harmonies.

The musical setting and the textual content comment upon each other. The harmonious tonal music reinforces the idea that the way of non-resistance, of the love of enemies, is good, beautiful, sublime. A timeless, unsurpassed ethic set to timeless, unsurpassed musical harmony, like "intimations of a paradisiacal garden."[18] (For its part, eighteenth-century harmony receives the profound

[18]As we heard Paul Hillier comment above. (*Arvo Pärt*, 35)

validation of Christ's loving commandment.) The way of revenge is first introduced by Bach's prelude played *backwards* at a frenetic speed, and then is set either amid serial rows or shouted in deliberate cacophony, so that a morality that Christ identifies as crude and outdated is set to a crude atonality that itself is destined to be outdated. Mutual tribute for Bach and Christ, mutual condemnation for a petty and vengeful morality, and modern tonality/atonality.

* * *

It is not entirely accurate to associate Pärt's eight-year impasse with a consciously-felt spiritual crisis. The seeds of his faith convictions did inform his 1960s compositions and were deleterious to his relationship with the State. His spiritual search also played a profound role in his life during the "silent" period and in his way out of it. But he did not stop composing as the result of a spiritual impasse. It would be more fruitful to consider the significant role of the spiritual pursuit *during* Pärt's transition period, for it was during precisely those years that his journey to the Orthodox Church was taking place.

That journey, as described earlier, was bound up together with his search for meaning in monophonic melody, his discovery of early music and especially chant, and his gradual realization that their foundations lay in prayer. Ascetical texts, mostly from the Christian East, were finding their way to him during this time. Concomitantly, he was on a journey toward marriage to Nora, after each had joined the Church.

So his compositional silence was less associated with a spiritual crisis than with a spiritual transition. In the late 1960s his heart was becoming spiritually attuned, oriented toward Christ, and certainly drawn to the Western musical tradition and its settings of sacred texts—but he didn't yet feel he had a definitive spiritual home. He began to internalize sacred texts and sacred arts through his deepening prayer life and a growing spiritual life.

Music Found in Silence

Pärt's eight years of transition were characterized by an involuntary silence. Yet they led him to a new kind of quietude that would now come to characterize the music itself.

The Music of Silence

> *How can one fill the stillness*
> *with notes that are worthy of this silence*
> *—this stillness that has just passed?*

Given the broad dynamic range and diverse character of Arvo Pärt's music, it is interesting to note how often the words "silence" and "stillness" come up when it is described by his listening public, by performers, and by music critics. Here too there is a natural kinship with ECM Records, who have used the slogan "The Next Best Sound to Silence," and all of whose recordings since the 1990s begin with five seconds of silence.[19] There are two elements at play, which we will investigate here: stillness *in* the compositions,

---

[19]See John Kelman in All About Jazz, October 31, 2011. The 2011 documentary film "Sounds and Silence: Travels with Manfred Eicher" (directed by Norbert Wiedmer and Peter Guyer) is highly illuminating about Eicher's vision and his relationship with silence.

namely the actual spaces between notes; and the quietude *of* the compositions, or the ethos of silence that his work seems to exude. These may operate together or separately. Together, they create a sense that the music has emanated from silence—and furthermore of a particular kind that is discernible within the music.

Music begins and ends with silence. Paul Hillier makes a point that is at once self-evident and profound: "Music is a negation of silence, but depends upon it for differentiation from a surrounding world of sound."[20] This can pertain to the beginning and ending of a piece—how the piece as a whole differentiates itself, as sound. Some of Pärt's works begin and/or end in ways that call particular attention to the silence, either bursting right in (*Passio, In Principio,* and *Arbos*) or starting so gently that one can scarcely identify where the music has begun (*Te Deum, Stabat Mater,* and *Nunc Dimittis*). There are pieces that begin or end with rests—such that quiet is written into the opening and/or closure of the work (e.g., *Cantus*). In *Tabula Rasa,* after the last *pianissimo* E from the contrabass, the score dictates a full four and a half measures of stillness.[21] "Rests are rich in sound," says the composer succinctly.[22]

Then there is the hush found between the notes. Mozart is famously quoted as saying that "the music is not in the notes but in the silence in between." Debussy has made similar pronouncements;[23] so has the jazz trumpeter/composer Miles Davis, "The Prince of Silence," who endured his own compositional hiatus

---

[20]*Arvo Pärt,* 199.
[21]I.e., about a half-minute's worth, at the prescribed tempo.
[22]Restagno, 68.
[23]"Music is the silence between the notes." This famous quotation is unsourced.

during several years in the 1970s.[24] Each of these musical personalities, in his own particular way, belies an inner stillness that one does not sense in most other composers, even great ones. Paul Hillier speaks of how in some cases one feels the music is being lifted out of sound and into silence, a striking reversal of how one usually considers the relationship of the two.[25] Many of Pärt's works are punctuated by quiet, in ways that lift both the sounds and the stillnesses into our consciousness. Sometimes this is an effect of Pärt's music being so driven by text—by words and phrases, each separated by silence. That is the case, e.g., in *Passio* and *Miserere,* where most phrases are set in stark relief from utter quiet. This happens whether the texts are actually sung or mute (serving only as the piece's rhythmic and thematic structure).[26] Even some of the *tintinnabuli* works that bear no direct relation to a text, such as *Tabula Rasa* and *Fratres,* feature this kind of punctuation. Performers have spoken of their first glimpse of an Arvo Pärt score with the galling impression that there is nothing there to play! This is commonly reported about *Für Alina,* but also about *Tabula Rasa.* Nora Pärt describes the rehearsals for *Tabula Rasa*'s premiere as a fiasco—the performers had not the faintest idea of how to play the piece.[27] The score looks like gossamer—there is more space than substance. "Where is the music?" they asked.[28] It is indeed a work lavished with silence—such as

---

[24]"Music . . . is not the notes you play, it's the notes you don't play." His colleagues said about him that he ". . . always came from silence, the notes existing in a purity all their own." CD liner notes, to Keith Jarrett, Gary Peacock, and Jack DeJohnette, *Bye Bye Blackbird* (ECM 1467, 1993).

[25]*Arvo Pärt,* 199.

[26]See above at pp. 75–78.

[27]Restagno, 54.

[28]CD liner notes, *Tabula Rasa* (ECM 1275, 1984).

between the violin entrances in the opening movement "Ludus"—
as well as one sustained outburst of powerful sound, at the close
of that same movement.

Tabula Rasa is also an example of a piece that, even where there
is continual sound one senses an ethos of stillness. This is especially the case throughout the second movement, tellingly entitled
"Silentium." The aforementioned turbulent *fortissimo* at the end
of Movement 1 ("Ludus") makes the sad-but-hopeful calm of
Movement 2 ("Silentium") ring out all the truer. As unpromising
as the rehearsal was in Nora Pärt's recollection, she also tells of
the hush that followed the stunningly successful performance: "I
have never heard such a stillness as the silence in the hall at the end
of the work."[29] The audience's silence was reverential as well as
reflective of the character of the music's own sense of quiet, which
in turn reflected the inner stillness out of which the music came.
What they heard, and what we hear in *Tabula Rasa* is a calm that
knows the storm well and bears its marks, a silence that is all the
deeper for having been *earned*. This indeed could well describe
the composer's entire musical output after 1976, the *tintinnabuli*
period, after he had weathered the deep and protracted turmoil
of his silence and inner transition.

Composer James MacMillan remarks, "Every composer knows
that the pre-creative silence is not empty but pregnant with possibility." He continues, "It is presence as absence; absence as
presence; which is precisely what music is. The umbilical cord
between silence and music is the umbilical cord between heaven
and earth."[30] The roots of Pärt's work in that pre-creative silence
can sometimes be quite conscious and explicit. He says, about

[29]Ibid.
[30]MacMillan, "Divine Accompaniment."

Te Deum, "I had to draw this music gently out of silence and emptiness."[31] The composer sees himself as a midwife, birthing a living being out of the womb of quietness. The *Te Deum* belies just such a process: it begins nearly imperceptibly and ends almost as gently. But in this work, as with other *tintinnabuli* compositions, the genesis in silence characterizes the whole, through hushed and loud passages, simple and busy ones. As Pärt said in an interview over twenty-five years ago,

> Before one says something, perhaps it is better to say nothing. My music has emerged only after I have been silent for quite some time. Literally silent. For me, "silent" means the "nothing" from which God created the world.[32]

Stillness is something to be approached with love and awe, he continues, that it might give birth to music. Only then might it be *worthy* of the silence, rather than an intrusion upon it. In a later interview, he posed the rhetorical question, "How can one fill the stillness [. . .] with notes that are worthy of this silence—this stillness that has just passed?"[33]

Reduction

In one of Arvo Pärt's most frequently quoted aphorisms, he says, "I have discovered that it is enough when a single note is beautifully played."[34] He is describing—not the style or the method, but

---

[31]CD liner notes, *Te Deum* (ECM 1505NS, 1993).

[32]From an interview with Leo Normet published in 1988, cited in Jeffers Engelhardt, "Perspectives on Arvo Pärt after 1980," in Shenton, ed., *Cambridge Companion*, 29–48, p. 35.

[33]Restagno, 68.

[34]Richard E. Rodda, liner notes for *Arvo Pärt: Fratres*, I Fiamminghi, The Orchestra of Flanders, Rudolf Werthen (Telarc CD-80387, 1995).

the *topos* or "space" of *tintinnabuli*, something he feels he can enter, or "wander into." "Here," he says, "I am alone with silence." Plus, "*Everything that is unimportant falls away.*"[35] Reduction for Pärt is vital; it is the paring away of all that is inessential. This calls to mind Christ's words, "Every branch of mine that bears no fruit, he takes away, and every branch that does bear fruit he prunes, that it may bear more fruit."[36] *Tintinnabuli* presented itself to Pärt as a way out of the logjams of twentieth-century polyphony; more than this, it is a way into the essential. It was born "from a deeply rooted desire for an extremely reduced sound world."[37]

Here one must absolutely distinguish "reduction" from "simplification," and certainly from "minimalism." What we are talking about has more to do with concentration, the identification of what Pärt calls the "nucleus": "Reduction certainly doesn't mean simplification, but it is the way—at least in an ideal scenario—to the most intense concentration on the essence of things."[38] The falling away of the extraneous, through this focus on the essential, is more than simplicity-for-its-own-sake. It is distillation; the identification of archetype.

The musicologist Leopold Brauneiss speaks of Pärt's reductionism in spiritual terms that help codify the distinction between it and minimalism:

> Turning to the archetypal means a humble overcoming of the personal ego, which partly dies with the first step, to be

[35]Liner notes, *Tabula Rasa* (ECM 1275, 1984). Emphasis added.

[36]John 15:2. This verse comes in the context of Christ's saying "I am the true vine," set to music in Pärt's eponymous composition of 1996.

[37]Nora Pärt, cited in Smith, "Sources of Invention: An Interview with Arvo Pärt."

[38]Ibid.

born again in various contexts and relationship to fellow human beings and to God. The negative term "minimalism" cuts the significant second step from the reduction, which deprives it of its actual purpose.[39]

Listeners are quite capable of perceiving the difference. "Pärt is remarkable," writes Wilfrid Mellers, "because he found it necessary, and possible, to pare away so much, leaving the residue the more meaningful the more exiguous it had become."[40] Descriptions are as liable to mention "purity," "honesty," and "distillation." These are all of a piece with each other: a successful reduction to essentials will breathe silence. This is so in any art form, but it has a particular resonance in music. Music that is free from the extraneous—whether it is quiet or loud, simple or complex—has a better chance of striking a listener as emanating from deep silence, bearing its traces. Contrary to music that has been "reduced" to background or "elevator" music, this distilled music commands complete attention.

That silent quality of the music can be contagious: it can instill peace, clear clutter.[41] Latvian conductor and violinist Gidon Kremer famously spoke of Pärt's work as "a cleansing of all the noise that surrounds us."[42] This same pared-down quality, however, can also summon people to add more data to it, for good or ill. The fact that Pärt's listeners hear "space" or "silence" in his music is

[39]"Musical Archetypes: The Basic Elements of the Tininnabuli Style," in *The Cambridge Companion to Arvo Pärt*, ed. Andrew Shenton (Cambridge: Cambridge University Press, 2012), 52f.

[40]Mellers, *Celestial Music? Some Masterpieces of European Religious Music*, 271. See also Mellers' essay in the liner notes to *Arbos* (ECM 1325, 1987).

[41]See pp. 37–40 above.

[42]Cited in Lubow, "Arvo Pärt: The Sound of Spirit."

surely one of the reasons that so many filmmakers employ his music in their work.[43] Pärt's compositions—most notably *Fratres, Spiegel im Spiegel, Für Alina,* and *Cantus in Memory of Benjamin Britten* (i.e., his untexted works)—have contributed to the soundtrack in literally dozens of major films, and countless amateur videos on the Internet. True, the music is evocative, and it is perhaps no coincidence that during his earliest professional years he wrote dozens of film scores. Filmmakers' frequent use of his existing compositions likely stems from their sense that the music, whittled down to essentials, allows the room for their narratives. The music comes across as "silent" enough to give place to more sound, to more aural and visual data. Judging by how many YouTube videos have been made to *Spiegel im Spiegel* alone, it seems as though people almost feel compelled to "fill it in." As if the music itself were not enough. Or perhaps the silence embedded in the music is too much for them to bear.

There have in fact been some quite stirring and beautiful uses of Pärt's oeuvre in film and in dance. The most apposite applications of Pärt's work in other art forms are those which tap into the fundamental spirit of Pärt's music: they bear the traces of inner silence and "suchness." They tap deeply into the basic brokenness of the world—a brokenness that is penetrated by sheer beauty.

---

[43]Among the many studies of the use of Pärt's music in film, see Kaire Maimets-Volt, "Mediating the 'Idea of One': Arvo Pärt's Pre-Existing Film Music" (Estonian Academy of Music and Theatre, 2009).

Excursus: Silence in the Tradition

In the pages above we have touched on several aspects of silence as pertaining to Pärt's biography and to his musical output. These have included:

- *Silence born of crisis and suffering.* Pärt's transitional period from 1968–1976 featured protracted absences of compositional output, born of a creative impasse, political oppression, and a spiritual search.
- *Silence as both absence and presence.* As well as being understood negatively, as an absence of sound, quiet may be considered positively in terms of what it is, what it represents, and what it produces.
- *Silence as multivalent.* Stillness may be devastating, consoling, healing. It may be dumfounded, it may be intelligent.
- *Silence as productive.* A word or work may proceed from silence, and may reflect the character of that silence.
- *Silence as a quality.* Quiet may characterize a word, an act, a work of art, whether or not it is in fact quiet in any way measurable in decibels.

In all, we have been seeing how an un-chosen silence born of crisis led Pärt to a more intentional silence born of cultivation in spiritual discipline. The spiritual tradition that Pärt came to embrace during his transitional years itself has a good deal to say about silence, and I suggest that this is no coincidence: every one of the themes I have just listed has a particular expression in the Orthodox Christian tradition. I am not arguing that Pärt has consciously drawn on these ideas, and their configuration within Orthodox theology and life, to shape his work. But they are certainly relevant to him and his oeuvre. The absence of traceable causality does not rule out correlation, given Pärt's relationship to the liturgical services, texts, saints, and prayer life of the Orthodox Church. An exploration of these themes then can be fruitful in understanding his music. In that vein, this section will explore the notion of silence in the (mostly Orthodox/Eastern) Christian tradition. I invite you to join me on this excursion, as far as you would like to go, and see what might strike a chord of relevance.

Does silence exist?

People tend to understand silence as the absence of sound. For a person to be silent, it is the absence of speech and movement. Conceiving silence in terms of "an absence," where there is no sound or speech, raises at least two questions. One of these is practical: is there any actual possibility of escaping all sound? In the earth's atmosphere, one will always hear something. Silence is a relative concept—it is *less* sound, or it is the absence of what we readily identify as sound. The other question is more philosophical: if silence is defined by absence, we must ask whether silence actually *is* anything. If silence is defined by no-sound or no-speech, then sound and speech are the ontological baseline, the default.

It is the same thing when we speak of darkness as the absence of light. We can speak of a shadow as an absence of light, because we presume that light is everywhere except in the shadow. But does darkness exist as such, or only as no-light? Same question for evil, in the face of good. If evil is merely the distortion or privation of goodness, does it have being-in-itself? Several ancient philosophers and theologians suggested that it does not.[44] In this

[44]This idea is found in Plato as well as in several early Christian writers, notably Gregory of Nyssa, Dionysius the Pseudo-Areopagite, and Maximus

thinking, good is the ontological baseline: only good exists. Evil has no existence of itself; it is a parasite onto goodness.

Likewise then, silence is an ontological parasite onto sound or speech. Silence, darkness, evil, do not exist. Yet, as elusive as real silence and real darkness are, we know that they are somehow present. As is evil. We speak of a state of silence; we likely have some experience of evil. Even if pure silence is effectively unattainable without the complete loss of hearing, we know that it *is* something. Silence can be a welcome relief after a day of noise and clutter. Silence can be an unwelcome absence after the loss of a loved one. Silence can force us into reckoning with ourselves—a positive event that we may seek out, or an uncomfortable experience we strive at all costs to avoid. We may know of silence as a portent of imminent action—"the deep breath before the plunge."[45] It may be the orchestral conductor's initial upbeat, which contains within itself the character and life of the entire composition to follow.[46] And it may simply be an empty pause, devoid of any particular meaning. Silence is nothing; silence nurtures sound and act; silence is a powerful force; silence thunders. Silence is multivalent.

Sound and speech and noise are practically everywhere, and are also of a profoundly mixed character: life-giving, life-destroying, mundane. In the context of pervasive noise, silence is more than

the Confessor. A useful summary may be found in Marina Luptakova, "The Nature and Origin of Evil According to the Eastern Christian Church," in *The Ethics of Terrorism: Innovative Approaches from an International Perspective*, ed. Yakov Gilinskiy, Thomas Albert Gilly, Vladimir A. Sergevnin (Springfield, IL: Charles Thomas, 2009).

[45]Words of Gandalf to describe the deceptively calm state before the Battle of the Pelennor Fields, in J.R.R. Tolkien, *The Return of the King*.

[46]See Dorian Supin, "24 Preludes for a Fugue," (2002), from 15:15.

just an absence; it truly is a kind of presence. It is a "thing" or state to be pursued. Or, in the presence of greatness, of awe, we are "brought" to silence. So, if we talk about seeking silence, or being brought to it, we are effectively talking about it as a thing, a place, a presence.

Silence and darkness can also be understood in terms of potentiality. Light shines out of darkness. Words come out of silence. God's creative word "Let there be light"[47] represents both: his word comes out of silence, and makes light to shine *out of darkness*.[48] The silence, the darkness, were not things-in-themselves, but were those states *out of which something came*. The silence and darkness represent non-being, the *nihil* out of which the world was created, *ex nihilo*. They do not represent God, for God is Being, beyond silence and sound, beyond light and darkness. The early Christian doctrine of *creatio ex nihilo*, that the universe was created out of nothingness, with no pre-existing matter, was a vital way of establishing the radical distinction between the created cosmos and the uncreated God.[49] As such, whether or not they have "ontological status," they are indispensable as ways of distinguishing things that are from things that are not. Even as we experience the sights and sounds of the created world, we must realize that if there were only light, if there were only incessant sound and speech, there would be blinding light, an absence of perspective, and indistinguishable cacophony. Leonardo da Vinci famously pointed out that, without shadow, we would be unable to see in perspective:

[47]Genesis 1:3.

[48]2 Corinthians 4:6.

[49]See Peter C. Bouteneff, *Beginnings: Ancient Christian Readings of the Biblical Creation Narratives* (Grand Rapids, MI: Baker Academic, 2008), *passim*.

Shadow is the obstruction of light. Shadows [are] of supreme importance in perspective, because, without them opaque and solid bodies will be ill defined; that which is contained within their outlines and their boundaries themselves will be ill-understood unless they are shown against a background of a different tone from themselves.[50]

These are some of the themes we will be looking at in the pages below, in terms of the texts and rites of the Christian tradition. We will see that while these sources display a cognizance of the many characters of silence, they are particularly interested in the role of silence within the relationship between human beings and God.

God's Absence

O Lord, be not silent! O Lord, be not far from me!

For people of prayer, divine silence, especially in the face of a desperate plea for help, can be devastating. Psalms and petitions frequently beg God *not* to be silent, for that silence would mean more than simply being ignored: it would be the withdrawal of consolation, of guidance, the retraction of life itself.[51] Silence and darkness characterize "the place of death," in Hebrew tradition, *Sheol.* So the Psalmist says, "If the Lord had not been my help, my soul would soon have dwelt in the land of silence."[52] Divine judgment against the nations includes the terrifying rebuke: "Sit

---

[50]§111 in his notebooks. Cited in Sean Cubitt, *The Practice of Light: A Genealogy of Visual Technologies from Prints to Pixels*, The Leonardo Series (Cambridge, MA: Massachusetts Institute of Technology, 2014), 171.

[51]E.g., Psalms 35:22, 109:1; Isaiah 64:12; Psalm 35:22; Psalm 94:17.

[52]Psalm 94:17

in silence, and go into darkness, O daughter of the Chaldeans!"[53] This theme is familiar to many Christian authors East and West,[54] and when Jesus cries out from the Cross: "My God, My God, why hast thou forsaken me?" he is quoting Psalm 22:1.

Yet silence as auguring God's withdrawal comes with an important proviso: that God is actually never truly absent. This conviction too is part of the tradition in the Psalms, notably in number 139, which consists entirely in the assurance of God's pervasive and sustaining presence: darkness is shown to be filled with light (v. 12); likewise *Sheol* is filled with God (v. 8). St Silouan of Mt. Athos explored this theme in his life and writings.

St Silouan, who had experienced the Spirit's presence, felt all the more His absence, which became the defining theme of his spiritual odyssey during his decades in the desert of Mount Athos. Knowing intimately the warmth, the life, the consolation of the Spirit's presence as Grace, made the Spirit's withdrawal all the more devastating. A considerable portion of Silouan's writing explores this anguish; his sustained meditation "Adam's Lament" serves as a searching allegory for a universal human loss.[55] St Silouan's work was furthered by his disciple and biographer Archimandrite Sophrony, of the Monastery of St John the Baptist, in Essex, England. Sophrony too has a great deal to say about the phenomenon of "God-forsakenness."[56]

[53]Isaiah 47:5. See John Breck's essay "Silence, Stillness and Listening to God." (http://johnrbreck.com/silence-stillness-and-listening-to-god)

[54]A notable example from the West is the great sixteenth-century Spanish mystic St John of the Cross, in his *The Dark Night of the Soul.*

[55]Sakharov, *Saint Silouan the Athonite*, 448–456.

[56]See Nicholas V. Sakharov, *I Love Therefore I Am: The Theological Legacy of Archimandrite Sophrony* (Crestwood, NY: St Vladimir's Seminary Press, 2002), 171–197.

Silouan and Sophrony emphasize that God never actually forsakes anyone, nor does he sever the ties of communion between himself and his creation. Sophrony especially stresses that the silence experienced during periods of "God-forsakenness" consists of God's withdrawing our ability to perceive Grace. Theologically speaking, it is impossible for God ontologically to absent himself from any part of his creation. But his allowing us to *sense* his desertion may be a case of God's providential guidance, leading toward a fuller awakening to his actual presence. As such it may constitute a significant stage in the spiritual life.

St John Climacus speaks of our experience of forsakenness as an opportunity for the expression of genuine love, in a state of bright sadness:

> When a baby starts to recognize its father, it is filled with happiness. If the father has to spend time away on business before returning home, it has its fill of joy and sadness—joy at seeing the one it loves, sadness at the fact of being deprived so long of that same love. Sometimes a mother hides from her baby and is delighted to note how sadly the child goes about looking for her and stirs up the flame of love for her.[57]

Apart from this dynamic of "perceived forsakenness," silence—as quiet, as stillness—can also bespeak the divine *presence*. In a passage in 1 Kings that strikingly describes God's appearance to Elijah,[58] the narrative emphasizes that there were many great portents, such as rock-splitting winds, earthquake, fire, as elsewhere

---

[57]eds. Colm Luibheid and Norman Russell, trans., *John Climacus: The Ladder of Divine Ascent*, Classics of Western Spirituality (New York: Paulist, 1982), 143.

[58]1 Kings 19:9–12

in the scriptures.[59] But these were not where God was. Where was God, and from where did he speak? The Hebrew is *qol damamah daqqah*, lending itself to several possible translations involving "voice" or "sound" (*qol*), "stillness/motionlessness" or "silence"(*damamah*), and "small" (*daqqah*). While the RSV renders the divine presence as "a still small voice," the NRSV translation more arrestingly has God appearing within *"a sound of sheer silence."*

This suggests that stillness, which may seem to intimate God's absence, may also present an occasion in which God makes himself known. This partly has to do with our own silence, for one must quiet oneself to be alert to the divine. As the psalm has it, "Be still, and know that I am God."[60] The latter depends upon the former; the knowledge of God is contingent upon our stillness. We will say more on that subject later. But the flip side of the conscious building of silence is the way that God's presence suddenly stuns people into the silence of awe.

Awe before God

> Be silent, all flesh, before the Lord;
> for he has roused himself from his holy dwelling.

In the scriptures, the epiphany of God is not something that summons loquaciousness. Once God has shown himself, the human reaction can scarcely but be a humbled, stunned silence. The dissonance, between the uncreated, all-powerful and all-knowing God, and the created, contingent, and fallen human being, is a very great one. In Judeo-Christian thinking, a human being cannot

[59]E.g., Exodus 19:16; Isaiah 6:4; Ezekiel 1:4, Job 38:1.
[60]Psalm 46:10.

even properly *survive* the undiluted vision of God.[61] The revealed presence of God brings one into an immediate awareness simultaneously of God's unfathomable greatness, and of one's own insignificance and brokenness, as when Job cries. "I had heard of thee by the hearing of the ear, but now my eye sees thee; therefore I despise myself, and repent in dust and ashes."[62] That same prophet, on hearing from God himself about his creating and sustaining every aspect of creation, can only say, "Behold, I am of small account; what shall I answer thee? I lay my hand on my mouth."[63] It is one thing to study God or discuss him, and another to encounter him.

"Be silent, all flesh, before the Lord; for he has roused himself from his holy dwelling," commands the prophet Zechariah.[64] The idols, notes the prophet Habakkuk, are stone-silent, without breath, without the potential to speak profitably to anyone. But stone-silence is precisely the appropriate posture before the divine: "But the Lord is in his holy temple; let all the earth keep silence before him" (Hab 2:18–20). Intelligent, word-bearing creatures must therefore mimic the dumb stones.

The scriptures and the Orthodox Christian liturgical tradition speak of a particular awe before the divine, as manifested in the crucified Christ. Here, humans and angels alike are struck dumb as they behold the inconceivable wonder: the Son of God—fully divine, great-beyond-greatness, the creator of the universe—not only becomes a vulnerable human but submits himself to death. Thus, we sing on the eve of Easter:

[61]Exodus 33:20.
[62]Job 42:5.
[63]Job 40:4.
[64]Zecharias 2:13.

> Let all mortal flesh keep silence,
> and in fear and trembling stand;
> for the King of kings and Lord of lords
> comes forth, to be slain,
> to give Himself as food to the faithful.[65]

Again we would note the irony of opening our mouths and sing-ing—about being silent. But like everything we do liturgically, our silence before the crucified and entombed Lord is meant to mirror the attitude of the angels, who also sing, and are also struck dumb by the sight:

> The spiritual powers and the angelic hosts
> Stand in silence, overcome with wonder
> Before the awesome mystery of your tomb.[66]

The angels, whose praise is traditionally understood as ceaseless (a perpetual recitation of "Holy, Holy, Holy") stand in silence.[67] Does the sound of their ceaseless praise actually cease?

The Psalms tell us that, with the angels, the entirety of creation, even the stars and planets, praise God. They do so silently, but with an endlessly resonating voice. The thoroughness of that inner contradiction has to be read, verse by verse, to be believed:

> The heavens are telling the glory of God; and the
> firmament proclaims his handiwork.
> Day to day pours forth speech, and night to night
> declares knowledge.

---

[65] *Cherubikon*, Divine Liturgy for Great and Holy Saturday.
[66] Stases of Holy Saturday Matins.
[67] Revelation 4:8. See also the *Te Deum* hymn: "Tibi Cherubim et Seraphim incessabili voce proclamant: Sanctus, Sanctus, Sanctus . . ."

There is no speech, nor are there words; their voice is
   not heard;
Yet their voice goes out through all the earth, and their
   words to the ends of the universe.[68]

The psalms are here picking up an age-old theme: that the cosmos itself generates harmonious music. The idea of the "music of the spheres" discussed in the last chapter, based on the Pythagorean perception of the relationship between physics, mathematics, and music, was taken up directly by Plato, and subsequent Jewish, Pagan, and Christian thinkers. Of particular interest here is the fourth-century Christian father St Gregory of Nyssa. Gregory writes of the human body as the instrument through which the soul makes its music.[69] That idea is interesting enough, but goes deeper: the human composition is but a microcosm of the entire universe, itself "a diverse and variegated musical harmony."[70] The link between human and cosmic harmony/music is deep, and has its roots in God who is the composer and choirmaster. God creates the universe as a great chorus, a dance that interprets his song. The human person is a distillation of that musical creation, who, through falling into sin, now distorts the song and can be re-tuned only in Christ.[71] The heavens, indeed, tell the glory of God, through their silent music. And humans can too, with the music of their life, as well as through the music they make.

* * *

[68]Psalm 19:1–4.
   [69]*On the Making of Humanity*, §9, i (*Patrologia Graeca* [henceforth, *PG*] 44, 149B); cf. also *On the Soul and the Resurrection* (*PG* 46, 29A).
   [70]*On the Inscriptions of the Psalms* I.3.xix. See Ronald E. Heine, trans., *Gregory of Nyssa's Treatise on the Inscriptions of the Psalms* (Oxford: Oxford University Press, 1995), 89.
   [71]Ibid., III.6.lx (in Heine pp. 138f).

And so the contradictions abound. God's silence is not truly God's silence. Our awestruck silence is something that we speak and sing about. The angelic silence seems not to interrupt their ceaseless praise. And the stars and planets praise God silently with a voice that is heard to the ends of the universe. Human attempts to describe God, and the life in pursuit of him, are bound to embrace paradox. This is because we seek to describe indescribable realities. Accepting or wrestling with paradoxes can be a part of the journey: they can function like the Zen *koan*, jarring us out of the complacent belief that we understand the world and can grasp its suchness. Of such things is the silence of God, and human silence before God.

Silence That Speaks

The collected Sayings of the Desert Fathers includes the following anecdote: some monks ask the great Abba Pambo, "Say something to the archbishop, so that he may be edified." Abba Pambo replies, "If he is not edified by my silence, he will not be edified by my speech."[72] Monks throughout history have enjoyed taking bishops down a peg. Here is an archbishop who apparently needs some attention, but Pambo seems to consider him a hopeless case and takes a pass. He gives us a paradigm of silence as instruction, for those who are prepared to hear it. Compare the example of the monk who did not need Abba Anthony's spoken words: "It is enough for me to see you."[73] A person may exude teaching and wisdom without saying a thing.

[72]Benedicta Ward, trans., *The Sayings of the Desert Fathers: The Alphabetical Collection* (London: Mowbray, 1975), 69. See also *Give Me a Word: The Alphabetical Sayings of the Desert Fathers*, trans. John Wortley, Popular Patristics Series 52 (Yonkers, NY: St Vladmiir's Seminary Press, 2014).

[73]Ibid., 6.

The whole created world is capable of noiselessly revealing the truth about God. Hence the ancient practice of the contemplation of the created world—in Greek "φυσικὴ θεωρία/*physike theoria.*" In the clear conviction that God indwells the entire universe, and that God's own invisible nature is discernable within it,[74] the great Christian mystics would meditate upon the beauty of creation in order to discern the divine hand. This practice has Christian ascetical and theological roots that go long and deep. Ancient and modern mystics frequently meditated upon the glory of the universe as a testimony to the exponentially greater glory of the creator. Here is a relatively modern example that draws on an ancient one. The eighteenth–nineteenth-century writer/anthologist Nikodemos of the Holy Mountain writes about contemplating the heavens:

> The mind, by exercising its rational thought, can wonder at the order, the size, the beauty, the light, and all the other attributes of the sky. And in all of these, the contemplative person can see the wisdom, the creativity, the power and the beauty of him who created it. He can thus reason and say: If the sky which is created is so beautiful, so full of light, how much more beautiful and more luminous is the creator of the sky? . . . And so the mind climbs as high as it possibly can to the knowledge of the creator, and with this knowledge the mind excites the heart with the will to love this creator. St Basil [fourth century] encouraged us to think such thoughts, and through them to rise from the visible to the invisible and from the ephemeral to the eternal.[75]

[74]Cf. Romans 1:20, "Ever since the creation of the world his invisible nature, namely, his eternal power and deity, has been clearly perceived in the things that have been made."

[75]In Peter Chamberas, trans., *Nicodemos of the Holy Mountain: Handbook*

The seventh-century writer St Maximus the Confessor made a particularly elaborate and enduring case for how God may be perceived within created things. Maximus said that God creates the world according to principles, or ideas ("λόγοι/*logoi*"). Creation, then, consists in the ideas of God actualized. The result is that to see the world truly, in its very silence, is to behold God's self-revelation. Contemplating nature, we contemplate the actualization of God's ideas. We are beholding divine thought incarnate.[76]

The Silence of Christ

Ancient and modern Christian writers have understood the life and death of Jesus Christ in terms of a thundering silence. As we have already seen, in Christian tradition Jesus is understood as God's Word,[77] God's perfect self-expression. Ignatius of Antioch speaks of Jesus Christ as "the Word that came forth from silence (ἀπὸ σιγῆς προελθὼν) . . ."[78] He is "spoken" into the silence of creation. When this eternal Son/Word took on human composition, the earliest Christian authors called it an act of "self-emptying" (in Greek, "κένωσις/*kenosis*"). The idea that this eternally divine person, the world's creator, chooses to become a time-bound, mortal creature who is vulnerable to his creation, is endlessly profound: doing so was an act of unfathomable *detachment*. According to

of *Spiritual Counsel,* Classics of Western Spirituality (Mahwah, NJ: Paulist Press, 1988), 71.

[76]For a basic introduction to the *logoi,* see Andrew Louth, *Introducing Eastern Orthodox Theology* (Downers Grove, IL: InterVarsity, 2013), 41–43.

[77]John 1:1–14.

[78]*Magnesians* 8.2. See in Bart Ehrman, trans., *The Apostolic Fathers I,* Loeb Classical Library 24 (Cambridge, MA: Harvard University Press, 2003), 248.

Philippians 2:6, Christ did not count his own divinity as something to be attached to, or "grasped." Christ, the eternal Son of God, becomes the time-bound son of Mary, subject to all that could befall a human being, all the way to death. It was an act of renunciation, of reduction, of self-silencing.

There are many notable silences recounted during Jesus's life. Some of his acts are bookended with stillness: among these are the quiet within which he listens to the woman caught in adultery. There, the evangelist takes note that the moments both before and after Jesus speaks ("Let him who is without sin cast the first stone")[79] are marked by wordless action. Some of his most significant self-revelations are followed by a conscious silence. For example, after telling his disciples to walk in the light, and to become children of light, he departed "and hid himself from them."[80] Then, his speechlessness before his accusers on the way to his crucifixion represents many things: it was a fulfillment of prophecy,[81] an embodiment of his own teaching of non-resistance ("Do not resist one who is evil."[82]), and an active example of his revolutionary injunction to love one's enemies.[83] The gospels report Jesus's silence before the authorities as a conscious choice, for as the Divine One he had the option of obliterating his enemies.[84] His silence helped propel him onto the cross, which was

---

[79]John 8:6–8.

[80]John 12:36.

[81]See Isaiah 53:7. "He was oppressed, and he was afflicted, yet he opened not his mouth; like a lamb that is led to the slaughter, and like a sheep that before its shearers is dumb, so he opened not his mouth."

[82]Matthew 5:39.

[83]"Love your enemies and pray for those who persecute you" (Matthew 5:44).

[84]Matthew 26:53.

the whole point: he knew it was the cross that would inaugurate salvation.

And then there is what the ancient Christians understood as the most profound quiet of all: the silence of Christ crucified. The apostle Paul identified this in the mid-first century as "the word of the cross,"[85] another iteration of "silent speech." We have heard already of the hush of the angels before the crucified God himself. Jesus' silence on the cross, broken only by a few key phrases, follows from the silence that led to it. This self-emptying detachment of Christ is a mainstay of Christian reflection since the first century. The twentieth-century Roman Catholic theologian Hans Urs von Balthasar also reflects in depth on Christ's silences.[86] He speaks of Christ who, as he utters the cry to the Father, "surrenders himself into the Father's mute hands . . . the wordless but still resounding Word."[87] On the cross, Balthasar continues, "Jesus works not only by speaking but also by being silent, and anyone who follows him in this can learn from his silence, for it is a meaningful silence, like God's."[88] That is, with his last words from the cross, "it is finished," Jesus enters the hush of Sheol—a silence that engenders the thunderclap of the resurrection.

---

[85] 1 Corinthians 1:18.
[86] See e.g., *The Glory of the Lord: A Theological Aesthetics, Vol 7: Theology—The New Covenant* (San Francisco, CA: Ignatius Press), 142–161.
[87] M.T. Skerry, trans., *Christian Meditation* (San Francisco, CA: Ignatius Press, 1989), 41.
[88] Ibid., 42–43.

Hesychia: The Inner Disposition of Stillness

> *To be silent and to be, is better*
> *than to speak, and not to be.*

"Be still and know that I am God."[89] Within the context of Psalm 46, this well-known pronouncement functions as a reassurance that amid external and internal tumult, one may remain quiet in the knowledge that God is God. One may remain still and know that he will act.[90] In the context of the wider biblical and patristic tradition, this statement means yet more.

The scriptures and early church's writings place paramount importance upon the knowledge of God. To know God, how he acts, and what are his ways and his laws, is the paramout prize. It is sweeter than honey, more precious than gold.[91] It is the highest wisdom.

> Whoever fears the Lord will do this, and whoever holds to the law will obtain wisdom. She will come to meet him like a mother, and like the wife of his youth she will welcome him. She will feed him with the bread of understanding, and give him the water of wisdom to drink.[92]

Knowing God ensures stability of life.[93] And the way to that knowledge is through quiet. "Be still before the Lord, and wait patiently for him."[94]

---

[89]Ps 46:10.

[90]Exodus 14:14.

[91]Cf., e.g., Ps 19:7–10; Ps 119:103. See also Peter C. Bouteneff, *Sweeter Than Honey: Orthodox Thinking on Dogma and Truth*, Foundations Series (Crestwood, NY: St Vladimir's Seminary Press, 2006), 39–44.

[92]Sirach, 15:1–3.

[93]Ps 1:2–3.

[94]Ps 37:7.

In the post-biblical tradition, renunciation and silence quickly became understood as indispensable to the discipline of apprehension of truth, of self, of the divine. The sayings of many of the great Eastern ascetics underscore the role of quiet as part of renunciation and detachment, in the attainment of understanding. Silence is a lifeline to actual being, but easily disrupted by incautious speech: thus the second-century saint Ignatius of Antioch says, "To be silent, and to be, is better than to speak, and not to be."[95] Diadochus of Photiki (fifth century) says, "Spiritual knowledge comes through prayer, deep stillness and complete detachment. . . ."[96] Abba Moses (fourth century) says, "Sit in your cell, and your cell will teach you all things."[97] Basil the Great (fourth century) likewise writes, "Stillness initiates the soul's purification."[98] Peter of Damaskos (twelfth century) sums it up: "Stillness alone engenders the knowledge of God."[99]

One rather practical way in which this is understood is that in order to be filled with God, one must first become empty. So that the word/sound of divine knowledge can enter, one must keep silence. The Orthodox Church sings of the fourth-century ascetical saint Hilarion: "Christ beheld your pure and tranquil life, your meekness and silence. Therefore He made His abode in you and you became a divine dwelling."[100]

---

[95]Ephesians 15:1–2. In Ehrman, trans., (Loeb) 234, translation altered. Ἄμεινόν ἐστιν σιωπᾶν καὶ εἶναι, ἢ λαλοῦντα μὴ εἶναι.

[96]*The Philokalia*, Vol. 1, 255.

[97]Apophthegmata, Moses 6.

[98]*Ep.* 2, ii.

[99]Palmer, Sherrard, Ware, eds., *The Philokalia*, Vol. III (London: Faber and Faber, 1984), 107.

[100]Matins Aposticha, feast of St Hilarion (celebrated annually on October 21).

Two terms need introducing here, common as they are to the Greek-speaking Christian ascetical writers. One is "intellect," which is a limited translation of a much richer Greek word, νοῦς/ *nous. Nous* signifies a combination of mind, heart, soul, intellect. The other word is "stillness," specifically a cultivated stillness of mind and body. The Greek word is ἡσύχια/*hesychia*.[101] The ascetics believed that intellect needed to be tended and purified by stillness. The following is typical:

> You must purify your intellect (*nous*) completely through stillness (*hesychia*) and engage it ceaselessly in spiritual work. For just as the eye is attentive to sensible things and is fascinated by what it sees, so the purified intellect is attentive to intelligible realities and becomes so rapt by spiritual contemplation that it is hard to tear it away. And the more the intellect is stripped of the passions and purified through stillness, the greater the spiritual knowledge it is found worthy to receive. The intellect is perfect when it transcends knowledge of created things and is united with God . . .[102]

In modern times, asceticism and renunciation have come to connote manifestations of a dour, joyless disposition. The pursuit of self-understanding and the knowledge of God does indeed involve considerable mourning, as we come increasingly to recognize our own brokenness and the fallenness of the world. But it is also joy,

[101]"Hesychia" is the root of the word "hesychasm," which describes the practice of prayer in inner silence, in the renunciation of thoughts, passions, and images. A "hesychast" is a monastic who has committed his/her life to this practice.

[102]"A Discourse on Abba Philimon," in Palmer, Sherrard, and Ware, eds., *The Philokalia*, vol. 2 (London: Faber and Faber, 1981), 345. (cited in P. Sherrard, *Athos: The Holy Mountain* (Woodstock, NY: Overlook Press, 1982), 160).

as we will see later. Here is a telling meditation by the eleventh-century Greek mystic Nikitas Stithatos:

> Stillness is an undisturbed state of the intellect, the calm of a free and joyful soul, the tranquil unwavering stability of the heart in God, the contemplation of light, the knowledge of the mysteries of God, consciousness of wisdom by virtue of a pure mind, the abyss of divine intellections, the rapture of the intellect, intercourse with God, and unsleeping watchfulness, spiritual prayer, untroubled repose in the midst of great hardship and, finally, solidarity and union with God.[103]

Stillness, Reduction, and Monologic Prayer

Stillness requires stilling. Before one talks about the ultimate goal of "solidarity and union with God in h*esychia*" one must actually work to be emptied of inner noise. The more one is able to achieve internal quietude, the less susceptible one will be to outer tumult: a genuine inner silence is ever accessible, as much in the peace of the desert as the cacophony of the city. But again, one must simplify. One must reduce. And the more one pares away the inessential in the self—in inner dialogue, in way of living, the direction of one's eyes—the more attuned he or she will be to the essential.

The fifth-century desert ascetic Abba Arsenius heard a voice tell him: "Arsenius, flee, be silent, pray always, for these are the source of stillness."[104] This typical saying links inner peace with silence

---

[103]Nikitas Stithatos, "On the Inner Nature of Things" §64, in *The Philokalia*, vol. IV, 125.

[104]Benedicta Ward, *The Sayings of the Desert Fathers: The Alphabetical Collection* (London: Mowbray, 1975), 8.

and prayer, reminding us that a consistent instrument in the attainment of *hesychia*, especially as practiced in the Christian East since at least the fourth century, has been brief, simple, repeated prayer. Such prayer, sometimes called "monologic" when reduced to the repetition of a single word or phrase, has its roots in several scriptural passages: Jesus himself says that in prayer, people ought not "heap up empty phrases" in the hope to "be heard for their many words."[105] The idea is that we needn't try to impress God, ourselves, or each other with lengthy improvised words addressed to him. What is more, extemporaneous prayers risk missing the mark as to who God even is, what creation is, and who we are. In its recommended private prayer practices as well as its communal prayer life, the Orthodox Church has always relied exclusively on established, tested prayer texts. In church services and during some set times of prayer, these texts may be long and complex. But in daily life, whether still or active, monologic (short and repetitive) prayer is prevalent and, at least since the sixth through eighth centuries, it is usually "The Jesus Prayer."

The Jesus Prayer in its basic form runs, "Lord Jesus Christ, Son of God, have mercy on me." There are many variations: For instance, the words "a sinner" can be added to the end, but some compress it even further. The curtailing can continue to the point where one simply repeats the name "Jesus."[106] Prayer thus distilled leaves the maximum freedom for God to act. The prayer eschews giving him instructions or describing him. The invocation of his name in itself has power.[107] The praying person acknowledges his/her utter

---

[105]Matthew 6:7.

[106]Just such a reduction, and then expansion, may be found in the first ode of Pärt's composition *Triodion* (1998).

[107]See, e.g., Philippians 2:9–11; Acts 4:12; Acts 8:12; 1 John 5:13; also Psalm 68:4.

contingency and complete dependence on God for our being. This simplicity lends itself to cyclic repetition and can act as a hushing mechanism for inner chatter. It can become the mind's default setting, a center of stillness from which the human psyche becomes unencumbered, and thus truly open and free. Diadochos of Photiki, again, writes:

> When we have blocked all of its outlets by means of the remembrance of God, the intellect requires imperatively some task which will satisfy its need for activity. For the complete fulfillment of its purpose we should give to the intellect nothing but the prayer "Lord Jesus." . . . Then that name implants in us a constant love for its goodness, since there is nothing now that stands in the way. This is the pearl of great price, which a person can acquire by selling all that he has, and so experience the inexpressible joy of making it his own.[108]

Such forms of prayer exist in other faith traditions. For example, practices associated with the Second Temple Judaism of the early centuries CE offer close comparisons. Monologic prayer has sometimes been compared to the *mantra* of other ancient Eastern faiths, not without reason.[109] In Hinduism and Buddhism the practice of the repetition of a phrase can be part of spiritual disciplines having to do with centering and silencing the mind/heart/body. Some mantras have no meaning in themselves, some do; some are similarly addressed to deities. The most significant

---

[108]"On Spiritual Knowledge" 59, *The Philokalia*, Vol. 1, 270. See Matthew 13:45–46.

[109]See, e.g., Christopher D.L. Johnson, *The Globalization of Hesychasm and the Jesus Prayer: Contesting Contemplation*, Continuum Advances in Religion (New York and London: Continuum, 2010).

factor that distinguishes the Jesus Prayer from a mantra is that, however it may function within the human mind and body, its content is grounded in the name of the person of Jesus Christ, who is understood as the Son of God; the prayer is addressed *to this person*.[110] Even as it serves to quiet, to center, and to ground a person's mind, soul, and body, its chief function rests in the human person's addressing the divine-human person of the Son of God. It is converse; it is *prayer*, pared down to its essence. Prayer, silence, stillness—all contribute to each other's development.

Silence and What Proceeds from It

> *Intelligent silence is the mother of prayer.*

Stillness and silence are so interconnected with wisdom that it is possible to mistake all silence for wisdom. "Even a fool who keeps silent is considered wise; when he closes his lips, he is deemed intelligent."[111] So we return to the fact that silence is neutral; silence is multivalent. The ancient writers will often qualify the silence that they praise and seek, speaking of *intelligent* silence, *timely* silence. "Intelligent silence is the mother of prayer," writes John Climacus.[112] "Timely silence . . . is precious, for it is nothing less than the mother of the wisest thoughts," writes Diadochus.[113] In order to think correctly, in order to have communion

[110]The Jesus Prayer is featured in J.D. Salinger's novel *Franny and Zooey*, where we get a reminder of how easy it is to misdirect that prayer. Zooey at one point remarks, "If you're going to say the Jesus Prayer, at least say it to Jesus. . . . Keep *him* in mind if you say it, and him only, and him as he was and not as you'd like him to have been." (Page 168 of the 1961 edition.)

[111]Proverbs 17:28.

[112]*Ladder of Divine Ascent*, 11.3.

[113]*The Philokalia*, Vol. 1, 276, quoted in Nouwen, 53.

and converse with God in prayer, one begins with not just any silence, but a right silence. Otherwise, what kind of prayer, what kind of communion with God will result?

> Let my prayer be counted as incense before thee,
> and the lifting up of my hands as an evening sacrifice!
> Set a guard over my mouth, O Lord,
> keep watch over the door of my lips.[114]

These psalm verses are central in the daily evening prayers of the Orthodox Church. The idea is that for prayer to be beautiful, rising like incense, one must keep a conscious stillness, a good silence. And so we are back to an observation from earlier in this section: a word will bear the characteristics of the silence whence it came.

The deeper the silence, the deeper the word. Dutch-born Catholic priest, academic and author Henri Nouwen has said, "Silence is the home of the word. Silence gives strength and fruitfulness to the word. We can even say that words are meant to disclose the mystery of the silence from which they come."[115] He goes on to indicate the importance of words in building the relationship of communion, between ourselves and all of creation, between ourselves and God. However, "Words can only create communion and thus new life *when they embody the silence from which they emerge.*" For,

> As soon as we begin to take hold of each other by our words, and use words to defend ourselves or offend others, the word no longer speaks of silence. *But when the word calls forth*

---

[114]Ps. 141:2–3.

[115]Henri Nouwen, *The Way of the Heart: Desert Spirituality and Contemporary Ministry* (San Francisco, CA: Harper & Row, 1981), 48.

the healing and restoring stillness of its own silence, few words are needed: much can be said without much being spoken.[116]

Catholic writer and mystic Thomas Merton has expressed similar ideas. "The mercy of God is not heard in words unless it is heard, both before and after the words are spoken, in silence."[117]

Words, sounds, music, proceed out of silence. The whole universe proceeds out of silence. And what a silence!

Creation from Silence

> *My Word that goes forth from my mouth*
> *will not return to me empty.*

However the early Christians understood the story of the six days of creation that we read in Genesis 1,[118] they placed considerable emphasis on the role of God's creative word: "Let there be . . .". We may note that, according to the Bible, the whole universe is created by speech. But not much speech. Each creative day begins with a simple divine utterance, but these "days" are thought by some ancient writers to have lasted eons.[119] And then, the seventh-day rest—essentially *stillness*—becomes enshrined as a part of the creative act as well. Silence thus bookends the entire generative process, as well as each day/act of creation. Is it possible even to fathom the depth of the silence which produced the creative word?

[116]Ibid., 57. Emphasis mine.

[117]Thomas Merton, "Philosophy of Solitude," in *Disputed Questions* (New York: Farrar, Straus, & Cudahy, 1960), 181.

[118]On the diversity of understandings among early Christian writers, see Bouteneff, *Beginnings*.

[119]E.g., 2 Peter 3:8. See also *Jubilees* 4:29, Justin Martyr *Dialogue with Trypho* 81, and Irenaeus *Against the Heresies* 5.23.2.

This is partly a theological problem: What is there before the creative word? Can we even speak of it as silence? Given that the genesis of the world involves the creation of time, what comes "before" time, other than an oxymoron? There is no space/time existence, no "is," in the sense that we know "is." Scientists, who note that it is illogical to speak of time or space before the Big Bang, confirm what the Fathers have already pointed out. For the theist, there is only God, who is outside the world, not of the world, not a part of the universe, but existing outside it. God is outside of time, beyond time and beyond timelessness. Beyond being and beyond non-being. We can only speak of "silence" before the creative word "Let there be . . .", because we know of the word, the sound. Where does it come from? It comes from "not-sound."

There is not, and then there is. There is no-word, and then there is word. The soundlessness is the divine silence, which (as noted above) contains within itself all the principles, ideas, purposes according to which the universe is made. "My Word that goes forth from my mouth will not return to me empty; it shall accomplish that which I purpose and succeed in the thing for which I sent it."[120] If a word or sound bears the character of the silence whence it came, is it possible even to ponder the nature of that silence whence proceeds the word generating the universe?

There is a difference between the uncreated silence of the creator God, and the noiselessness we know in the world he created. Yet if we could even fathom God's silence, it would serve as the model of the "intelligent silence" spoken of by John of the Ladder. It is that stillness that bears simultaneously the dumbstruck awe of God's

[120]Isaiah 55:11.

Icon of St John the Theologian "in silence."
Russian, *circa* first half of eighteenth century.
See p. 130.

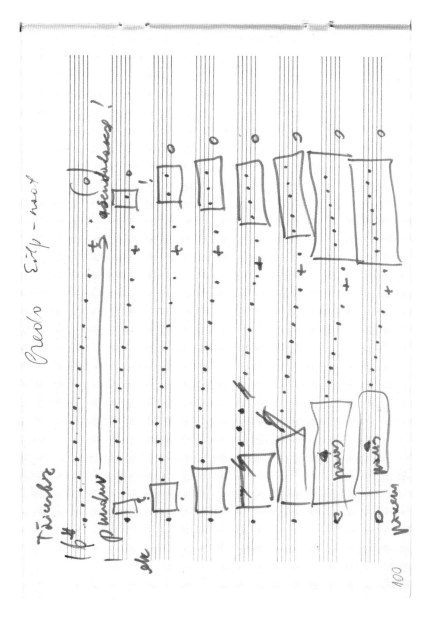

Unpublished pages from Arvo Pärt's musical diaries, November 1976. Outline for the composition *Summa* (1977), a setting of the Nicene Creed.
Courtesy of the Arvo Pärt Centre.

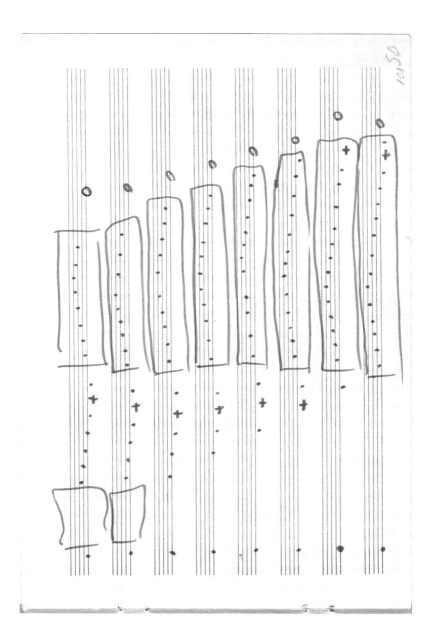

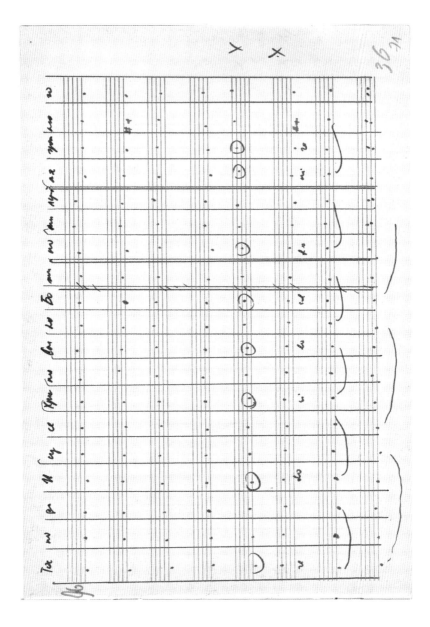

Unpublished page from Pärt's musical diaries,
May 29, 1976. Melodies to the Jesus Prayer.
Courtesy of the Arvo Pärt Centre.

Conferral of the degree Doctor of Music, *honoris causa* by Tikhon, primate of the Orthodox Church in America and president of St Vladimir's Orthodox Theological Seminary. May 31, 2014. Courtesy of Leanne Parrott Photography.

Onstage at Carnegie Hall.
Photo © Eleri Ever.

Tallinn Chamber Orchestra, Estonian Philharmonic Chamber Choir,
Tõnu Kaljuste, Carnegie Hall, performing *Adam's Lament*, with supertitles.
May 31, 2014. Photo © Eleri Ever.

Carnegie Hall, rehearsal. May 31, 2014.
Photo © Eleri Ever.

Estonian Philharmonic Chamber Choir with Tõnu Kaljuste, performing *Kanon Pokajanen* at the Temple of Dendur, Sackler Wing, Metropolitan Museum of Art. June 2, 2014. Photo © Stephanie Berger.

From left: St Vladimir's Seminary chancellor Fr Chad Hatfield, Arvo Pärt Project co-directors Nicholas Reeves and Peter Bouteneff, Arvo Pärt, Metropolitan Tikhon, seminary trustee Tatiana Lapchuk Hoff, and seminary dean Fr John Behr. Photo © Stephanie Berger.

Arvo Pärt and Metropolitan Tikhon at
Carnegie Hall reception. Photo © Eleri Ever.

Arvo and Nora Pärt, with the author.

presence and the cultivated stillness (*hesychia*) that is unruffled by interior or exterior noise. This is the silence of preparation, ready to listen to God's word, so that—filled with his sound—one may pronounce life-giving words akin to the divine.

The Silence and Music of Heaven

Heaven is where there is only life,
and therefore all that is not music is silence.

We have been reflecting on the capacity of silence to generate a word, a sound, an act. Once it has done so, the silence and the sound are in relationship with each other. The act testifies to, and therefore proves the quality of the silence. This relationship translates into that between our wordlessness and our words for God. The God of Judeo-Christian tradition is inconceivable and indescribable, and must be approached in silence and darkness—the early Christian writers called this *apophasis*. Yet it has been given to humans to say something, to him and about him, which they called *kataphasis*. The great mystical theologian Dionysius the Areopagite (probably from the sixth century) has explored this paradox thoroughly, speaking of God as "nameless, and yet having the names of everything that exists."[121] Dionysius asserts that God, who is beyond being, is found within the "dazzling darkness of a hidden silence."[122] Yet he notes the paradox that, given the way we are created, we must ultimately say something about God—so long as it is in the full cognizance of God's radical

---

[121]*The Divine Names* (PG 3, 596C). See in Colm Luibheid, trans., *Pseudo-Dionysius: The Complete Works,* Classics of Western Spirituality (Mahwah, NJ: Paulist Press, 1987), 56.

[122]*Mystical Theology* (PG 3, 997AB), in Ibid., 135 (translation altered).

otherness and ineffability. The affirmations (words) about God must bear the character of the negations (silences).[123] "Every affirmation . . . has the force of a negation pointing toward transcendence."[124] The *purpose* of silence is to generate a right word, a right sound. There is not the one without the other: no silence without sound, and no sound that does not begin or end with, or somehow embody, silence.

Singing in Praise of Silence

We are back to the paradoxes of the "sound of sheer silence," the absence/presence of God, and our intoning hymns about remaining wordless. We find these same kinds of oxymorons repeatedly in the language employed by the Church in praise of her saints. In one particularly striking example, we have St John the Theologian. He is the evangelist of the Word (John 1:1–14), who is regularly called "the son of thunder" in the poetic praise about him. Yet traditional iconography often portrays him with his hand gently placed over his mouth.[125]

That gesture suggests many things, one of them being that for John to pronounce his life-bearing words, he must first be silent. As Job had said, on his encounter with God, "Behold, I am of small account; what shall I answer thee? I lay my hand on my mouth" (Job 40:3). This icon is frequently referred to as "St John in Silence." But note that the configuration of his fingers form the four letters "ICXC," an abbreviation for "Jesus Christ," a frequent iconographic sign, and the gesture used in every Orthodox liturgy

---

[123]Even if, as Dionysius elsewhere asserts, God is beyond both the affirmations and the negations, beyond words, beyond silence.

[124]*Epistle* 4, (PG 3, 1072B), in op cit., 264f.

[125]See first page of color insert.

by the clergy giving blessings. The hand both draws attention to a mouth that speaks, but also diverts attention to something greater, which is the Word, Christ himself. The image portrays the evangelist as silent but for his testimony to the Word.

The Church sings about John the Theologian in terms of both storm and silence:

> With your tongue resounding as thunder,
> you declare the hidden Word of the Wisdom of God!
> Beloved of God, you open your mouth to cry:
> "In the beginning was the Word!"
> Illumining all mankind with the knowledge of God.[126]

Only one other saint in the Orthodox church has been accorded the title, "the Theologian," the fourth-century Gregory of Nazianzus. The hymn sung in his praise resembles that to the gospelwriter:

> Your mind was not overwhelmed,
> while you searched the depths of the abyss of God
> to draw out the pearl, most noble Gregory.
> You devoted your silence to the Master, as much as your
> words.[127]

Without that silence devoted to God, there would be no words. But without the words, what would the silence be for? Because quietude, we will recall, can be either sterile or full of potentiality.

The following is taken from a hymn for St John Cassian (fifth century), which speaks first of his (preparatory, perspicacious) speechlessness, then his words:

[126]Vespers hymn at "Lord I call," Feast of St John the Theologian (May 8).
[127]Matins Canon, Feast of St Gregory the Theologian (January 25).

You watched and observed silence, venerable one.
Later you spoke out in words and deeds,
in humility, meekness and innocence,
as a prophetic and eloquent herald![128]

As we contemplate the interdependence of words and silence, we should now turn to how they relate to music. The Church praises many of the saints, but especially these theologians, as musicians or as musical instruments, as "harps of the spirit." Here is another hymn about John the Theologian:

Divinely inspired lyre for the songs of heaven,
whose secrets he wrote down for us,
singing wonderfully the song of songs.
with words from his mouth as music from a lyre,
he prays for us to be saved.

. . . musical instrument of wisdom, temple of the Spirit,
voice bringing the light of grace
brilliant and treasured eye of the Church![129]

And another about Gregory the Theologian:

The shepherd's flute of your theology
drowned out the trumpets of the rhetoricians.
For having searched the depths of the Spirit
the gift of eloquence was graced to you.[130]

---

[128]Vespers hymn at "Lord I call," Feast of St John Cassian (February 29).
[129]Vespers hymn at "Lord I call," Feast of St John the Theologian (May 8).
[130]Apolytikion (Troparion) for St Gregory the Theologian (January 25). See also the hymn at the Canon for the Feast of the Three Holy Hierarchs (January 30):
　　The ones who spoke for God were pillars of virtue and wisdom.
　　When they were silent or when they spoke; when they watched or
　　　listened,

Two of the most revered hymn-writers of the Church are Romanos the Melodist (sixth century) and John of Damascus (eighth century). John is called "A well-tuned organ and sweet-sounding harp."[131] The hymns about Romanos call him "The musical harp of the divine Spirit, the flute of the Church, the nightingale, the cicada, chanting the hymns of God." He is "the sweet-sounding harp which has as strings the words of the Spirit, singing and teaching openly to the ends of the earth, glorifying the brightness of God!"[132]

We are quickly coming to see that beautiful theology—in other words, theology that has emerged from an intelligent silence—is likened to the creation of music. The link between music and silence has been made before: sometimes more than any other sound, music and silence are capable of evincing truth and beauty, speaking of the heavenly and the divine. We think once more of English philosopher Aldous Huxley's observations on music, echoed earlier by Manfred Eicher, that other than silence, it bears the greatest hope of expressing the inexpressible. Words can be useful in lending precision, but they may also bring us to confusion.

Scottish minister and author George MacDonald has spoken of Heaven as "the regions where there is only life, and therefore *all that is not music is silence*."[133] C.S. Lewis's ingenious character

they commanded us by their words and deeds to cry:
Blessed are You, God of our Fathers!

[131]Vespers hymn at "Lord I call," Feast of St John of Damascus (December 4).

[132]Vespers hymn at "Lord I call," Feast of St Romanos the Melodist (October 1).

[133]"The Hands of the Father," in *Unspoken Sermons* (London: Strathan, 1867).

the devil Screwtape abhors both quiet and music, and so seeks to fill the world with meaningless noise:

> Music and silence—how I detest them both! How thankful we should be that ever since our Father entered Hell . . . no square inch of infernal space and no moment of infernal time has been surrendered to either of those abominable forces, but all has been occupied by Noise—Noise, the grand dynamism, the audible expression of all that is exultant, ruthless, and virile—Noise which alone defends us from silly qualms, despairing scruples, and impossible desires. We will make the whole universe a noise in the end. . . . The melodies and silences of Heaven will be shouted down in the end. But I admit we are not yet loud enough, or anything like it. Research is in progress.[134]

* * *

In the pages above we have reflected upon silence:

- that emanates from sound and turmoil.
- that has come from the awesome presence of God.
- that is cultivated as an inner state or temperament.
- that produces sound.
- And sound that reflects the character of its silence.

In constructing this section of my book, I could have reversed its two main parts: first talking about silence in the Eastern Christian tradition, and then about Arvo Pärt's biography and his music, making all the tidy linkages. My choice to do it the other way round was deliberate: first look at the composer and how silence

[134]C.S. Lewis, *The Screwtape Letters* (San Francisco, CA: Harper Collins, 2001), 119–120.

has informed his life and his music, then hear the voices from tradition, and see if these inform our understanding of his life and deepen our apprehension of his music. I would suggest that several crucial aspects of the composer's life and work resonate with what we heard from the ascetical fathers: his cultivation of stillness, his inclination toward reduction in pursuit of the essential, and especially his alertness to the ongoing interpenetration of joy and sorrow—the subject of this book's next section.

Perhaps the main overarching point common to the Christian reflection and Pärt's odyssey would be the relationship between wordlessness and word, silence and sound, stillness and creation, reflected in how the silence of Pärt's transitional period preceded the word, the way, and the music of *tintinnabuli*. In the pages to follow we will hear the Pärts speak of the birth of that new mode of conceiving music as "the Big Bang of creation." Equating his artistic development with the genesis of the universe may sound like a delusion of grandeur, but the metaphor is apt: tintinnabuli came as it were "ex nihilo," out of nothingness, in a way that could not have been predicted. And yet it carries with it a trace of the "nothing," the space, the stillness it came from. And subsequently it feels as if his compositions all emanate from and bear the quality of that silence.

* * *

I am reminded here of a sermon I once heard about the "Great Fast," the forty-day period of Lent that precedes the celebration of Easter. The homilist, seeking to evoke the concept of an intentional and subdued preparation, seized on the metaphor of bells. Very big bells. There are peals in Russia that are so large and so celebrated that they have names and are associated with patron saints.[135] They are respected almost as persons. The largest ones are so big that one cannot simply grab hold of the clapper and ring them at will. The sounding of such a bell has to be preceded by a process of steadily enlarging the radius of the sway. It takes considerable time and strenuous, focused effort. It begins with a gentle push by several people, then a gradual coaxing into greater and greater swings; one hears a whooshing sound as the enormous brass clapper begins to describe a larger and larger arc, until it finally finds purchase, making contact with the bell's side. People who have been near such a bell when the clapper strikes speak of a profound visceral effect, a seismic change of atmosphere, a multisensory event of strange beauty "heard" by the whole person, which often provokes weeping.

The Great Fast, said my homilist, was like that: seven weeks of gentle pushing, in quietude, patiently watching and following the swing that somehow involves both our effort and a powerful momentum that now lies outside ourselves. And then comes Easter: the great resonant peal of the resurrection.

The coming of something beautiful into the world is a matter of cultivation. It is sometimes a matter of intense labor: physical, emotional, spiritual. Speaking to artists of all kinds about the creative process, I have noticed that very few will attribute their works to their own brilliance alone. They may acknowledge their inner struggle, their manifest work, but they will also speak of "inspiration," perhaps from something outside themselves that they had nothing to do with. Some speak of God.

[135]Some useful background may be found in Elif Batuman, "The Bells: How Harvard Helped Preserve a Russian Legacy," *The New Yorker*, April 27, 2009.

Arvo Pärt's years of ferment, largely silent, can with hindsight be seen in terms of cultivation, something akin to the swinging of the bell's clapper. It was tracing its arc, in motion all along, sometimes through gentle pushes, sometimes propelled by anguished struggle, often without a clear destination in view. Looking back over the years, we can say that this was neither an absence of sound and music nor the forsakenness of God. His was a productive silence that ended up generating a sound that stilled the musical world and continues to resonate. That sound is in turn infused with silence, a worthy, intelligent silence, whence it came and whither it goes.

III: Bright Sadness

Печаль моя светла—My sorrow is bright.
Alexander Pushkin[1]

"What earthly sweetness remains unmixed with grief?" Thus begins a hymn by an eighth-century Christian theologian and poet.[2] Life is indeed bittersweet. Calling attention to the inevitably mixed, multiform experience of our existence might seem self-evident and un-profound, but not for long. Questions about the interweaving of joy and sorrow usually begin by asking why there is suffering in the first place, and why there is death, why evil. These questions, asked seemingly since the dawn of ideas, have taken philosophers, artists, and other inquirers down varied paths. Some have attributed life's vicissitudes to a basic sense of seasonality. The ancient wisdom of Ecclesiastes, dating centuries before the Common Era, tells us that there are seasons for laughter and for weeping, a time to mourn and then to dance, a time to break down and a time to build up.[3] The perceived cyclic character of favor and disfavor can also be a matter of maintaining balance: the religious concept of Karma speaks to the inherent equilibrium of the cosmos and

[1]From his poem, На холмах Грузии лежит ночная мгла . . . ("Upon the Hills of Georgia").

[2]St John of Damascus. This line begins a series of hymns sung at the Orthodox Christian funeral service.

[3]Ecclesiastes 3:3–4.

the play of cause-and-effect, with or without divine intervention. Others see a still more deliberate mechanism at play, where suffering can contribute to physical and spiritual development: the harrowing, strenuous, challenging periods of life play a role in establishing a more enduring joy and wholeness. A deeper, lasting happiness, not to mention wisdom, is earned through sorrow and struggle. Then there is the idea that in order to gain something you have to give it up, and so again it is a matter of loss and hope, with the aim of healthy detachment. All of these explanations of the fluctuations between affliction and redemption hearken to a natural order evident in the way life's events and experiences unfold. Agriculture is a common metaphor, as in "Truly, truly, I say to you, unless a grain of wheat falls into the earth and dies, it remains alone; but if it dies, it bears much fruit."[4]

The banality of many popular expressions ("to get to heaven you've got to go through hell;" "no pain, no gain") has all but inured us to the profundity of what they actually suggest. They encapsulate ways of making sense of suffering and sorrow. Many traditions speak of moving *beyond* good and evil, transcending the cycles of suffering and happiness. These are commonly associated with Eastern disciplines of detachment and enlightenment (*nirvana*, *satori*), but they can also be found in the Christian (notably Eastern Christian) goal of "dispassion" (in Greek, *apatheia*). But dispassion, *nirvana*, and *satori* are states to be *attained*, generally through lasting and often arduous struggle.

The arts and the sacred traditions alike, where they are true to life as we know it, will often reflect this interweaving of sorrow and consolation, brokenness and wholeness. Much of the effect of Arvo Pärt's work derives from how it speaks to people's deepest

[4]John 12:24.

sense of the interpenetration of conflicting realities. This music says that there is no joy not tinged with grief, and no suffering beyond redemption. His compositions are never simplistic, however simply they may be structured. They are faithful both to the brokenness of the world and to our hopes for its transfiguration. They hold the two strands together, knitting them together inextricably in a kind of unity. 1+1=1: the strange math we will be discussing below, that is sometimes invoked to describe his music, speaks to that interweaving.

Listeners and critics have described Pärt's double strands through a variety of metaphors. Björk calls one voice "Pinocchio," making mistakes, bearing and inflicting pain; and the other "Jiminy Cricket," whose role is both to comfort the erring one, and keep him in line.[5] Arthur Lubow likens them to a toddler learning how to walk, and a mother accompanying at every step with outstretched arms, ready to correct and catch.[6] Each of these characterizations delights Pärt. "Yes, it is so!" he beams. Critics and observers have invoked other images for the two qualities held together in Pärt's compositions: One is the vulnerable, human, voice that is straying and sometimes pained, the other is the stable, divine or angelic voice that consoles. These two lines take expression in the simple melody + triad rule that constitutes the foundations of *tintinnabuli,* underlying nearly all his compositions after 1976. But Pärt has so internalized that rule that even in the compositions that barely adhere to this rule, or have dispensed with it, somehow still exude its two-fold spirit.

[5]Interview with Arvo Pärt, as part of a 1997 BBC documentary on "Modern Minimalists." This may be found on the Internet; at the time of this writing, the URLs are in flux.
[6]Lubow, "Arvo Pärt: The Sound of Spirit."

Joyful Sorrow, or Sorrowful Joy?

The capacity of art—especially great art—to reach people in their time of suffering is immense. Various "voices" or sensibilities can configure our perspective: are we talking about a small black spot on a radiant sun, or a lone star in a pitch-black sky? Joyful sorrow, or sorrowful joy? Or is it the yin-yang of equal representation and interpenetration?

Spiritual traditions have likewise played their role in configuring these two poles. The Eastern Christian faith held by Arvo Pärt is liable to shape the perception of them in different ways. When it speaks theologically, Orthodoxy consistently affirms that the world is at root good. It is fallen, distorted, but not depraved. Harmony and holiness are the starting point and the ending point, even as we live now in an ambiguous moment where the end, the "age to come," is both here already and not yet actualized. In its ascetical modality the Church is more likely to configure those polarities in terms of mourning, yearning: brightness within sadness. Metaphorically speaking, the mirror is so darkened that it can only barely reflect divine goodness.[7]

* * *

In Greek the idea we have been discussing can be expressed in one composite word, χαρμολύπη (*harmolypi*) and two in Russian, светлая печаль (*svetlaya pechal'*). Bright sadness has come to characterize especially seasons of abstinence, fasting periods. Great Lent[8] is the period of seven weeks during which many Christians choose to deny themselves certain pleasures and reduce

[7] I Corinthians 13:12: "For now we see in a mirror dimly . . ."

[8] See Alexander Schmemann, *Great Lent: Journey to Pascha*, rev. edn. (Crestwood, NY: St Vladimir's Seminary Press, 1974), 31–33.

distractions; the goal is to reorient priorities, to sensitize bodies and minds to deeper, quieter things. Great Lent provides a period of vigilance that will rightly prepare for the genuine and enduring joy of redemption. It is a chosen darkening of the night in order to brighten our perception of the stars. It is no exaggeration to say that nearly every spiritual discipline, Eastern and Western, promotes similar kinds of renunciation in order to redirect and sharpen the senses.

Imposed renunciation causes voluntary suffering, but obviously most human heartbreak and anguish is unchosen, by victims of violence, sickness, turmoil, loss. Although suffering is by definition unpleasant, in times of grace we may recognize its potential role in emotional and spiritual growth. So, although people don't usually seek them out, suffering, sadness, pain, are not states that they avoid at all costs. We pursue them vicariously by reading heartrending literature, looking at harrowing images, or listening to doleful music. We acknowledge, in some part of ourselves, that a life of undifferentiated bliss is simply not real life, nor will we experience any growth in it. We believe we will be enriched, and perhaps even made wiser for what we have undergone in times of despondency, struggle, or torment. "The heart of the wise is in the house of mourning . . . ," says the Ecclesiast.[9] Paul can even say, "We rejoice in our sufferings, knowing that suffering produces endurance, and endurance produces character, and character produces hope, and hope does not disappoint us . . ."[10]

Enter, again, Arvo Pärt's music. We have remarked that its ethos carries a particular resonance for those who are suffering acutely.

[9]Ecclesiastes 7:4.
[10]Romans 5:3–5.

But *everyone* is suffering. And so much of his music speaks to that. The message that many people "receive" from Pärt's music might, it seems to me, be condensed into something like this:

> I know that there is brokenness and terrible suffering in
>   the world.
> I hear you, and am with you in it.
> I also know that suffering is not the last word.
> The last word is light.

The "I" of this interpretation is either the composer or the music itself. Such a message is echoed, again, within any of a number of spiritual traditions. Yet, as we have been doing throughout this book's journey, we move from that potential universality to specificity of the Orthodox tradition, which has had a great deal to say to this composer. That tradition's particular expressions of the universal struggle to make sense of evil and suffering along with their potential intertwining with hope, joy, and wholeness.

In looking at the Tradition first, and at the music second, I am reversing the sequence that I used for the previous section: there is no particular life-story to tell here about Pärt, as there was in the case of silence. Add to this that we are here looking at a quality of his music whose analysis will arguably be enriched by a more in-depth consideration of the basic human realities that inform it.

Bright Sadness in the Tradition

The spiritual tradition of the Christian East is at its root biblical. Its earliest texts are scriptures shared among different Abrahamic faiths that narrate a "very good" creation,[11] describing paradise and its loss. In its Psalms, this scriptural tradition sets out the lamentations and strivings of a disconsolate people who still palpably hope for redemption in their God. It moves through what Christians identify as "the New Testament," most notably in the odyssey of Jesus Christ, whose voluntary death and descent into Hades is one continuous motion with his glorification and ascent. That biblical world has a long history of interpretation in the Eastern Christian church through the liturgies and texts, primarily in Greek and Syriac, but also in the writings of spiritual luminaries from other parts of the world, such as in the Slavic and Balkan regions. Some of the key themes we will be reviewing resonate deeply within Pärt's *tintinnabuli*.

We will begin with the Bible: the Genesis creation stories, the Psalms, and the Christ narratives, with a coda from the letters of Paul. We will proceed through some Eastern Christian ascetical and liturgical writings. Among these, we will consider a man whose thinking is particularly near and dear to Pärt, the twentieth-century monastic St Silouan the Athonite, as conveyed to us by his disciple the *staretz* Sophrony. Bright sadness, we will see, takes many forms, but runs as a deep and steady current throughout.

Genesis 1–3: Paradise Lost

The interplay of chaos and order, and fall and redemption, run deep in biblical tradition and begin at its beginning. In Genesis, God creates the world, taking note of its goodness at every stage.[12] The opening three chapters of Genesis narrate the creation of the

[11]See Genesis 1:31.
[12]Genesis 1:4, 1:10, 1:12, 1:18, 1:21, 1:25, and 1:31.

world *twice*, from two different perspectives. In chapter 1 we hear of the six days of creation. It is a cosmocentric account, describing the creation of the world as an ordered process, telling about the separations that made the world what it is: light from darkness, land from water, and so on.[13] It tells of the origin of living things, and the place reserved for humanity within this created order. The second story (roughly chapters 2 and 3) provides an anthropocentric account focused on the creation of humankind, and the relationship between humans and God.[14] Let us look briefly at each.

The first chapter of Genesis narrates the "Hexaemeron," six days of creation, each day/event producing a stunning cluster of creative activity set in motion by a tiny divine phrase, "Let there be . . .", uttered from within an eternal silence. Then, famously, on the seventh day, the Sabbath, God rests, lapsing back into silence.[15] This seven-day creation sequence gives theological weight to the seven-day week observed originally by the Babylonians (weeks ranging in length from three to ten days existed before the seven-day week became standard), so that it became the seven-day worship cycle of Jewish tradition, later adapted by Christians. If the silence "before" creation is inscrutable, ultimately describing the ineffable being of God, that of the seventh-day rest is a way of impregnating creation with silence, insuring that the rhythm and music of creation will be punctuated with rests, and reflect the stillness whence it came.

---

[13]Paul Beauchamp, *Création et séparation: Étude exégétique du chapitre premier de la Genèse*, Lectio Divina (Paris: Cerf, 2005).

[14]As it happens, the second story was probably written first. See, e.g., David Carr, *Reading the fractures of Genesis: Historical and Literary Approaches* (Louisville, KY: Westminster/John Knox, 1996.

[15]Genesis 2:3: "So God blessed the seventh day and hallowed it, because on it God rested from all his work which he had done in creation."

In this second story, often known as the Paradise narrative, we see the dynamic of glory and its distortion. If anything, the focus is less on the glory than on its being marred by human beings. God himself breathes life into the human beings, places them in a flourishing garden with what they need to sustain them. But before they are fully formed, the humans heed a foreign (serpentine) voice and disrupt the divinely decreed order by which their full glory would have come. They thereby inaugurate the whole dynamic of mortality, sin, and suffering. Although their mortal fate already comes with a promise of redemption,[16] they have set in motion a terrible series of declines. Adam, created in the divine image, now begets children in *his* tarnished image.[17] Cain murders Abel, death builds upon death. Even after the great flood and its cataclysmic "reboot" of creation, the people of Babel ignominiously fail in their attempt to build a tower that will let them reach God.[18]

In all we learn that the human person (*Adam* in Hebrew, *anthropos* in Greek) is created as good, moreover as a mirror of the divine. But human beings stumble and set a course of decline that affect the whole world. Beauty is disfigured, the image of God distorted. *But not hopelessly.* For God is at work to redeem fallen creation.

Through this lens, the rest of history becomes the story of the human appropriation of that redemption, through straying and being called back to the path. The mirror is being wiped clean again to reflect the ineffable glory of God. The cycle of glory, distortion, and restoration plays out through eons, centuries, years,

---

[16]Many Christians understand Genesis 3:15 as the "proto-gospel" (*protevangelium*), with its promise that the serpent will be crushed, that God does not forget his people.

[17]Genesis 5:1–3.

[18]Genesis 11:1–9.

days, seconds, nanoseconds. It takes place through the cosmos, in every locality, in every human heart, and in every grain of sand. At every moment and in every thing, we behold unspeakable beauty and brokenness. The conviction is that beauty is the actual truth, whereas brokenness is beauty that is distorted but not destroyed.

Unlike Christians, Jews did not (and still do not) see the story of Adam and Eve as the story of "the fall" of humanity. But Jews and Christians alike read Genesis 1–11 as a series of decline narratives—an avalanche of sin and what the biblical scholar Gerhard von Rad calls a "continually widening chasm between man and God."[19] And both traditions, in their respective ways, see these narratives as leading to the divine promise of redemption.

As for the Christian tradition, the hope embedded in the Genesis narratives takes place through a sense of the embeddedness of Christ himself in these narratives. This practice of "typology" begins from the first century of Christianity: Adam is understood as a "type" or reverse-image of Christ.[20] The tree of perdition in the garden of paradise is a "type" for the cross. The Sabbath day, on which God rests in the creative act, is a foreshadowing of the day of Jesus' day of rest in the tomb: "This is the most blessed Sabbath, on which Christ has fallen asleep to rise . . ."[21] Then there is the day of his resurrection, which the gospels call "the first day of the week,"[22] and which subsequent tradition calls the *eighth* day. This is the never-ending eighth day, which is

---

[19]*Genesis: A Commentary,* Second edn. (London: SCM, 1972), 152. See also Bouteneff, *Beginnings,* 7–8.

[20]See, e.g., Romans 5:14.

[21]Kontakion, Tone 6, from the Orthodox hymnography of Great and Holy Saturday.

[22]Matthew 28:1; Mark 16:2; 9; Luke 24:1; John 20:1; 19.

also the first day of the *new* creation.[23] Apart from the Christian typology, Jewish and Christian understandings coincide in the conviction that creation and redemption are one-and-the-same act of God. Salvation is set within the act of creation; creation *is* salvation.[24]

This biblical tradition thus calls us to hold together two sensibilities: one told from a timeless or eschatological perspective, where creation and redemption are one and the same, and one that respects the time-bound world that is our physical context, where creation and redemption are experienced quite separately, sometimes in isolation from each other. Yet, however one theologizes creation and redemption, whatever assurance we have that the world is redeemed, no Jewish or Christian spiritual master would deny that our life in the world is bound up with grief. Neither would he or she deny that we live in assurance of the resurrection, of God's redemption of his people, of the age where every tear is wiped from our eyes and where death is swallowed up for ever.[25] This is already an inaugurated reality—it is ours here and now. And yet we know there are tears. We know there is death.

The Eastern Christian tradition, reading the Genesis creation narratives through the light of Christ, come to particular conclusions, based on a set of fundamental presuppositions.[26] It is worth taking

[23]See St Basil the Great, *Homilies on the Hexaemeron* 2.8. All of this is explored fruitfully in Alexander Schmemann, *Introduction to Liturgical Theology* (Crestwood, NY: St Vladimir's Seminary Press, 1975), 59–67.

[24]See Bouteneff, *Beginnings*. 7–9; also André LaCocque, "Cracks in the Wall," in Paul Ricoeur and André LaCocque, *Thinking Biblically: Exegetical and Hermeneutical Studies* (Chicago: University of Chicago, 2003), 3–29.

[25]Isaiah 8:25; Revelation 21:4.

[26]My summary is an extrapolation from a broad constellation of sources. Further reading on these matters could profitably begin with John McGuckin,

a moment to set them out here, because they have everything to do with how a believing Orthodox Christian, or anyone in that church's praying orbit, is going to approach matters of loss and hope, fall and redemption, and joyful sorrow.

1. *The goodness of the world*

   We have taken note of God's repeated pronouncements of the world's goodness, as he is creating it. But even after the fall in the Garden of Eden, the universe, at its root, is still good. The ambiguity that comes through the fall does not obliterate that goodness in total depravity, or introduce a duality of gods or forces. Light and goodness are what truly exist. Darkness and evil do not—they are only shadows, veil over light and goodness, but have no actual existence in themselves. As John the Evangelist writes, "The light shines in the darkness, and the darkness has not overcome it."[27]

2. *The goodness of human nature*

   To reiterate, whatever was lost or distorted in the human fall, corruption was not complete either for the natural world or for humankind. Human beings are not totally corrupt, nor is redemption or perdition predestined. Distortion is not depravity; the way to regaining purity is universally available, owing to Christ.

3. *The inheritance of the fall*

   The human fall is tied up with the whole of creation, animate and inanimate. It sets into play a mode of living

"The Song of Creation," in his magisterial work, *The Orthodox Church: An Introduction to Its History, Doctrine, and Spiritual Culture* (Oxford: Blackwell, 2008), 204–210.

[27]John 1:5.

that is plagued by sin and death, along with the need for purification and redemption. Every human being is born into that complex and tortured dynamic, into the consequences of the fall. But no human being is born guilty, personally culpable for the fall.

4. *Death as the Way to Life*
The mixed, ambiguous, distorted world into which we are born is intimately known by God, who involves himself in its every particle. Jesus, the Divine Son, enters into it and subjects himself to its corruption—all the way to death. God implicates himself in the broken modality of existence that we all follow, and shows it to us in its fullest realization: suffering and death can bring goodness, reintegration. Not all suffering is redemptive, but there is no other way to bliss than through affliction. And death is no longer the last word: life is.

As we have seen, in the Church's theological thinking, the starting place is goodness. This is so in the Genesis account of creation, and somehow even in its recitations of human decline: the presumption is that goodness is the ontological default. They serve to emphasize that the vision of the good is accessible to us only in a veiled way, for our perception is marred, our compass decalibrated. We struggle, continuing to grope our way forward, in this "vale of tears" that is also a "vale of soul-making."[28] But God is good and has redeemed the world.[29]

---

[28] John Keats called the world "the vale of soul-making" in his letters. The term was more recently deployed in describing the understanding of good and evil in Irenaeus of Lyon, by John Hick; see his "An Irenaean Theodicy," in Stephen T. Davis, ed., *Encountering Evil: Live Options in Theodicy,* rev. edn. (Louisville, KY: Westminster John Knox, 2001), 38–52.

[29] John 16:33.

Broken but redeemed. Fallen but raised. Distorted but we see light. And all of this can be expressed conversely: The world is redeemed, but still suffering. We are raised, but we still die. We see light, but our eyesight is warped. Christians know how this all turns out—or at least that it turns out extremely well even though the world we inhabit continues to be deeply ambiguous.

Having explored these foundational biblical texts and what they have led to in later theology, let us continue our journey with the Psalms.

Psalms: Lament and Hope

> *The Lord is close to the brokenhearted*
> *and saves those who are crushed in spirit.*

The entire Hebrew Bible, we can say without exaggeration, is a balance of sin and redemption, of human straying and divine calling back, of lament and hope. We have seen how these are embedded within the creation and decline narratives in Genesis.[30] We see it in the odyssey of the ancient nation of Israel, enslaved, liberated, traversing deserts, chosen and yet sometimes seemingly forsaken by God, alternately faithful and unfaithful to him. We see it in God's rebuke of his disloyal people, and his constant fidelity and deliverance. The Book of Psalms, a cross-section of Israelite prayer-life, provides an evocative portrayal of the attitude of God's people toward him, themselves, and the universe. The prayers present us with a consistently dual disposition, an oscillation between dejection and sure hope of deliverance. Psalms of

---

[30]I use the word "narratives" without adjudicating whether they are historical or ahistorical. Based on my study of Genesis in the fathers (op. cit.), I believe that Orthodox theology can sustain either view.

lament unfailingly become psalms of divine praise, the movement from modality to the other sometimes taking place within a single verse.

The psalms are worthy of our reflection for the clarity and depth with which they evoke the spirit of bright sadness. But in addition to that, they have closely accompanied Pärt's life and work. He read them regularly during his transitional years; they inspired page after page of monophonic melody. He set psalms and psalm-verses to at least a dozen of his compositions.[31] We behold a remarkable harmony between the form of the psalms—accompanying grief to its fullest, and directing that grief toward hope—and the ethos of his music.

Old Testament scholars and sociologists have observed that the Psalms served an important function in the society's collective and personal suffering and grief, experienced through generations of struggle, war, and dashed national and religious expectations. For one, the psalms give voice to the full range of unvarnished human emotions. They do so in a dialogical context: emotion is put directly into relationship *with* God, expressed *to* God, in the knowledge that God is all-powerful, and will hear the plea.[32] The psalms simultaneously express that grief, legitimize it, and also delimit it, defining its proper parameters. Those who are suffering are thus given a particular place within society, their

---

[31]*Cantate Domino Canticum Novum, De Profundis, An Den Wassern Zu Babel Saßen Wir Und Weinten , Zwei Slawische Psalmen, Ein Wallfahrtslied / Pilgrims' Song, Psalom, Miserere, Como Cierva Sedienta, Cantique Des Degrés, Peace upon You, Jerusalem, Habitare Fratres In Unum, Drei Hirten-kinder Aus Fátima.*

[32]See Walter Brueggemann, "From Hurt to Joy, from Death to Life," *Interpretation* 28 (1974).

grief is "formed" or directed.[33] The laments in this way receive and accompany those who are suffering—even those who would address God with audacious questions and exasperated impatience. Early Christians turned to the psalms for the same reasons. The fourth-century saint Athanasius of Alexandria reflected at length on them. He concludes, "The one who hears also comprehends and is taught in [the Psalter] the emotions of the soul." He continues,

> In the Psalms it is written and inscribed how one must bear sufferings, what one must say to one suffering afflictions, what to say after afflictions, how each person is tested, and what the words of those who hope in God are.[34]

Let us focus for a moment on the weeping of the people of Israel: despair over their lowliness, their struggles, their decimation by enemies, and their detractors. Lament leads to petitions, and the petitions are uttered in the conviction that they will be heard. God will hear, God is great, God is a loving and redeeming God. Let us immerse ourselves for a moment into this three-part movement, one of the key structures in the psalms:

In Psalm 6, 1) the narrator's situation is dire, but 2) he gains the strength to drive away his enemies 3) based on his conviction that God has heard him.

> I am weary with my moaning;
> every night I flood my bed with tears;
> I drench my couch with my weeping.

[33]See "The Formfulness of Grief," *Interpretation* 31 (1977).
[34]Athanasius of Alexandria, "Letter to Marcellinus," in *Athanasius: The Life of Antony and the Letter to Marcellinus*, ed. Robert C. Gregg (New York: Paulist, 1980), 108f.

154

My eye wastes away because of grief,
it grows weak because of all my foes.
Depart from me, all you workers of evil;
for the Lord has heard the sound of my weeping.
The Lord has heard my supplication;
the Lord accepts my prayer.[35]

In Psalm 42, the writer 1) mourns as he is mocked, 2) casts his mind back to times he has rejoiced in God with a crowd of others and 3) that memory summons his hope.

My tears have been my food day and night,
while men say to me continually,
"Where is your God?"
These things I remember,
as I pour out my soul:
how I went with the throng,
and led them in procession to the house of God,
with glad shouts and songs of thanksgiving,
a multitude keeping festival.
Why are you cast down, O my soul,
and why are you disquieted within me?
Hope in God; for I shall again praise him,
my help and my God.[36]

In Psalm 56, the psalmist 1) begins in faith that God cares about his woes, so 2) he will protect him from his foes, therefore 3) he praises the Lord.

Thou hast kept count of my tossings;
put thou my tears in thy bottle!

[35]Psalm 6:6–9.
[36]Psalm 42:3–5.

Are they not in thy book?
Then my enemies will be turned back
in the day when I call.
This I know, that God is for me.
In God, whose word I praise,
in the Lord, whose word I praise,
in God I trust without a fear.[37]

In Psalm 102, the narrator 1) grieves over being forsaken, but 2) has faith in God's eternal nature, so 3) the timeless God will favor his people at this time.

For I eat ashes like bread,
and mingle tears with my drink,
because of thy indignation and anger;
for thou hast taken me up and thrown me away.
My days are like an evening shadow;
I wither away like grass.
But thou, O Lord, art enthroned for ever;
thy name endures to all generations.
Thou wilt arise and have pity on Zion;
it is the time to favor her;
the appointed time has come.[38]

In Psalm 116, the writer 1) sees that God healed his anguish, because 2) he remained true to God, and therefore 3) he will rejoice in his relationship with God.

For thou hast delivered my soul from death,
my eyes from tears,

[37]Psalm 56:8–11.
[38]Psalm 102:9–13

> my feet from stumbling;
> I walk before the Lord
> in the land of the living.
> I kept my faith, even when I said,
> "I am greatly afflicted";
> I said in my consternation,
> "Men are all a vain hope."
> What shall I render to the Lord
> for all his bounty to me?
> I will lift up the cup of salvation
> and call on the name of the Lord.[39]

Elsewhere, the pattern is more binary, a simpler movement from desolation to consolation, as in Psalm 126, where the poet writes,

> May those who sow in tears
> reap with shouts of joy!
> He that goes forth weeping,
> bearing the seed for sowing,
> shall come home with shouts of joy,
> bringing his sheaves with him.[40]

Likewise in Isaiah, "He will swallow up death for ever, and the Lord God will wipe away tears from all faces, and the reproach of his people he will take away from all the earth; for the Lord has spoken."[41] In the book of Revelation, the people are twice told the same thing: "For the Lamb in the midst of the throne will be

---

[39]Psalm 116:8–13. Christian liturgical use of this psalm focuses on the verse "I will lift up the cup of salvation, and call on the name of the Lord," as a sign of the cup of the Lord's Supper, i.e., the Eucharist.

[40]Psalm 126:5–6.

[41]Isaiah 25:8.

---

their shepherd, and he will guide them to springs of living water; and God will wipe away every tear from their eyes."[42]

The people know this. Their faith is in God, whose *nature* it is to hear and to redeem. They know him and have experienced his mercy. The word "steadfast" appears in the psalms as a descriptive for God's love over one hundred times, sometimes as a repeated refrain within individual psalms, as in "For his steadfast love endures forever."[43] God's actions in the world reveal him to be preternaturally merciful toward it. What is more, the love of God is especially directed toward those who are downcast. "The Lord is close to the brokenhearted and saves those who are crushed in spirit."[44] They describe a God who continually turns a special ear to the broken, the needy, the destitute. The idea, prominent in Liberation Theology, of God's "preferential option for the poor" is supported throughout the Psalms and the Prophets.

> For the Lord hears the needy,
> and does not despise his own that are in bonds.[45]

> "Because the poor are despoiled, because the needy groan,
> I will now rise up," says the Lord;
> "I will place them in the safety for which they long."[46]

---

[42]Revelation 7:17. See also Revelation 21:3–5: "and I heard a loud voice from the throne saying, 'Behold, the dwelling of God is with men. He will dwell with them, and they shall be his people, and God himself will be with them; he will wipe away every tear from their eyes, and death shall be no more, neither shall there be mourning nor crying nor pain any more, for the former things have passed away.' And he who sat upon the throne said, 'Behold, I make all things new.'"

[43]See Psalm 118 and especially Psalm 136.

[44]Psalm 34:18.

[45]Psalm 69:33.

[46]Psalm 12:5.

All my bones shall say,
"O Lord, who is like you?
You deliver the weak
from those too strong for them,
the weak and needy from those who despoil them."[47]

As for me, I am poor and needy,
but the Lord takes thought for me.
You are my help and my deliverer;
do not delay, O my God.[48]

With my mouth I will give great thanks to the Lord;
I will praise him in the midst of the throng.
For he stands at the right hand of the needy,
to save them from those who would condemn them to
    death.[49]

I know that the Lord maintains the cause of the needy,
and executes justice for the poor.[50]

"We are suffering, we feel forsaken, yet you are our sure hope, for you are our light and our salvation." The two-fold disposition of lament and praise comes to a particularly sharp expression in Psalm 22.[51] The extent of grief and suffering are great, to the point of being almost unfathomable. The psalm begins with the cry of forsakenness, a cry that is uttered both day and night. The psalmist is humiliated by enemies who are like animals—his world has

[47]Psalm 35:10.
[48]Psalm 40:17.
[49]Psalm 109:30–31
[50]Psalm 140:12.
[51]See Ellen F. Davis, "Exploding the Limits: Form and Function in Psalm 22," *Journal for the Study of the Old Testament* 53 (1992), 98.

collapsed completely. And all of this seems to be the work of God: "thou dost lay me in the dust of death!"[52]

The movement out of this mire begins with verses of plea:

> But thou, O Lord, be not far off!
> O thou my help, hasten to my aid!
> Deliver my soul from the sword,
> my life from the power of the dog!
> Save me from the mouth of the lion,
> my afflicted soul from the horns of the wild oxen![53]

It continues with vows to proclaim to others who God is and what he has done for his people, that they properly may praise him:

> I will tell of thy name to my brethren;
> in the midst of the congregation I will praise thee:
> You who fear the Lord, praise him!
> all you sons of Jacob, glorify him,
> and stand in awe of him, all you sons of Israel![54]

This praise of God is what closes the psalm—praise that is shown to radiate in circles ever moving outward, across space and time, to the ends of the earth, to foreign nations, even to those who are already dead, and to those who have not yet been born.[55] The psalm has truly plumbed the depth of despair and forsakenness, and brought it to unparalleled heights and depths of faith, proclamation, and praise.

---

[52]Psalm 22:15.
[53]Psalm 22:19–21.
[54]Psalm 22:22–23.
[55]Davis, "Exploding the Limits: Form and Function in Psalm 22," 96.

It is this very psalm which is quoted by Christ on the cross: "My God, my God, why hast thou forsaken me?"[56] With these words on Christ's lips, at his moment of severest agony, his witnesses—who know their psalms well—understand him as part of the history and tradition of Israel. As the biblical scholar Ellen Davis writes, "Jesus' cry belongs to Israel's public language."[57]

Christ and the Cross

Lo, through the cross joy has come into all the world.

The Christ of Christian faith—in his person, his teachings, and his death and resurrection—presents a definitive and holistic embodiment of the bright-sadness paradox, through a series of descents and ascents, of greater and larger degrees. As understood within a classical Christian theology, he traces a trajectory from the heights of heaven to the depths of hell, and back. Divinity (light, life, eternity) to humanity—dead humanity, to be exact—and back. Theologically speaking, this is about as great a bright-sadness motion as can be fathomed. John the Evangelist writes, "No one has ascended into heaven but he who descended from heaven, the Son of man."[58] The eternal and almighty one descended into human vulnerability, as an infant, then a child, then an adult, one who was tempted, who hungered and thirsted, and wept for his friends. He ascended the cross to descend into hell, to be raised into heaven.

Christ emptied himself of any attachment to his divinity, becoming a servant/slave in an occupied land; he submitted to death and was glorified:

[56]Matthew 27:46, Mark 15:34.
[57]"Exploding the Limits," 104.
[58]John 3:13.

Though he was in the form of God, [he] did not count equality with God a thing to be grasped, but emptied himself, taking the form of a servant. [. . .] he humbled himself and became obedient unto death, even death on a cross. Therefore God has highly exalted him and bestowed on him the name which is above every name.[59]

Right after his baptism in the Jordan River[60]—itself a descent and ascent—Jesus began his teaching with the Beatitudes in a way that mirrored the lament-praise cycle of the Psalms. These verses contrast the plight of the existential broken world with the age to come. It is a movement from longing and hunger to fulfillment and redemption.

> Blessed are the poor in spirit, for theirs is the kingdom of heaven.
> Blessed are those who mourn, for they shall be comforted.
> Blessed are the meek, for they shall inherit the earth.
> Blessed are those who hunger and thirst for righteousness, for they shall be satisfied.
> Blessed are the merciful, for they shall obtain mercy.
> Blessed are the pure in heart, for they shall see God.
> Blessed are the peacemakers, for they shall be called sons of God.
> Blessed are those who are persecuted for righteousness 'sake, for theirs is the kingdom of heaven.
> [. . .] Rejoice and be glad, for your reward is great in heaven.[61]

[59]Philippians 2:6–9.
[60]Mark 1:9–10 and parallels.
[61]Matthew 5:3–12.

The version in Luke's gospel is still more concise:

> Blessed are you poor, for yours is the kingdom of God.
> Blessed are you that hunger now, for you shall be satisfied.
> Blessed are you that weep now, for you shall laugh.[. . .][62]

These verses might be misunderstood as an assurance of a karmic reversal of fortune in an inaccessible distant future. Rather, this is the kingdom that Christ has already inaugurated, a kingdom that lives in a perennial tension with the broken reality that remains. That co-existence explains why our experience of the world is so deeply mixed: a bright sadness indeed. John the Evangelist quotes him as saying, "I have said this to you, that in me you may have peace. In the world you have tribulation; but be of good cheer, I have overcome the world."[63] Christ, light, life decisively prevailed over tribulation, darkness, and death.

This also means that, in the world as we know it—broken and redeemed—there is no way upward without first going downward. The way to brightness is through sadness. Jesus not only knew this, but completely implicated himself into that difficult reality by dying and rising, redeeming the world. His famous adage, taken from basic agriculture, that a grain of wheat must fall to the earth and die in order to produce fruit, illustrates the way of human life, and points also to what he himself was about to undergo. The way to glory is through the cross. According to John the Evangelist,

> Jesus answered them, "The hour has come for the Son of
> man to be glorified. Truly, truly, I say to you, unless a grain

[62]Luke 6:20–21.
[63]John 16:33.

of wheat falls into the earth and dies, it remains alone; but if it dies, it bears much fruit. He who loves his life loses it, and he who hates his life in this world will keep it for eternal life.[64]

There is a wealth of meditation on the mystery of the cross, or what Paul calls "the word of the cross"[65]—its message and meaning. For many of us today, the cross has lost all its ironic power: it is ubiquitous and therefore meaningless. Or it has become the symbol of an oppressive religion. The irony of the cross (an instrument of torture) becoming a herald of joy, a sign of victory, what an Orthodox liturgical text calls a "weapon of peace"[66] (the paradox is built right in to that expression), is such that it was a "scandal" and "stumbling-block" to the first hearers of Christian preaching.[67] It is difficult for us to recover that sense of how bizarre it was, to preach that the way of joy, light, salvation, heaven, was through the death by slow asphyxiation of a messianic preacher. This strange proclamation is sung weekly during the Orthodox Church's Resurrection Matins: "Lo, through the cross joy has come into all the world." It calls people to hold in tension the polarities of sorrow and joy.

Keep in mind that sorrow is not tragedy. As theologian David Bentley Hart points out, there is a tendency in some theologies to see in the cross a "tragic beauty."[68] Although this is yet

---

[64]John 12:23–25.

[65]1 Corinthians 1:18.

[66]This image is taken from the Kontakion hymn for the Feast of the Exaltation of the Cross, in the Orthodox Church.

[67]1 Corinthians 1:18; 1:21; 1:23.

[68]See "The Consolations of Tragedy, the Terrors of Easter," in David Bentley Hart, *The Beauty of the Infinite: The Aesthetics of Christian Truth* (Grand Rapids, MI: Eerdmans, 2003), 373–394.

another oxymoron, it misunderstands the logic completely. Not just because it can come across as banal (think of the faded rose, or the sad clown), but also because the cross is not a tragedy. Tragedy would be a person who dies unaware of the forgiveness of his beloved, or of God. *Sorrow* is what describes the creator of the world killed by his creation. Calling this event "tragic" undermines its life-bearing significance.

If there is a tragic element to the cross it is that it confirms the catastrophe of fallen human nature: that a person who spoke the truth and loved completely, was executed because of it. But the cross, in all its surrounding grief, is a radiant thing. Christ, dead on the cross, is God's gift of complete and total self-offering. As such the crucifix is the icon of the divine nature; it is God's self-portrait. But the cross is also the sign that all of humanity is brought to a completely new and exalted state. Christ is, after all, risen from the dead, and this changes everything.

In Orthodox hymnography, Jesus tells his weeping mother, "Do not lament me, mother, seeing me in the tomb. [. . .] for I shall arise and be glorified with eternal glory as God."[69] When the women who followed Jesus come to his tomb to pay their respects, they are greeted by an angel who says, "Why do you seek the living among the dead? Do not weep! Announce the resurrection to the disciples!"[70] The prophecy was fulfilled that said, "The Lord God will wipe away tears from all faces."[71] Christians carry this hope, this conviction, knowing that the crucifixion story ends in joy. It is done, it is consummated. But we still live in a world that has yet fully to actualize that ending.

[69]Canon of Great and Holy Saturday, Ode 9.
[70]Resurrection Matins Evlogeitaria hymn.
[71]Isaiah 25:8.

Our mourning is definitely not finished. But it is infused with faith, hope, and love.

Paul

Paul of Tarsus, whose epistolary writings predate the gospels, is the earliest known Christian writer. Without knowing the accounts of Matthew, Mark, Luke, and John, he received and shaped the "word of the cross" in indelible ways that often caught the curious mixture of grief and joy we are contemplating here. As it happens, a concentration of his observations on that score can be found in his second letter to the Corinthians. He writes with loving pastoral care to a community which on another occasion he had chastised for misbehavior and poor attitude. His opening oscillates between "affliction" and "comfort" (the Greek παρακαλέω/*parakaleo* may better be translated here as "consolation" or "encouragement"):

> Blessed be the God and Father of our Lord Jesus Christ, the Father of mercies and God of all consolation, who consoles us in all our affliction, so that we may be able to console those who are in any affliction, with the consolation with which we ourselves are consoled by God. For as we share abundantly in Christ's sufferings, so through Christ we share abundantly in consolation too. If we are afflicted, it is for your consolation and salvation; and if we are consoled, it is for your consolation, which you experience when you patiently endure the same sufferings that we suffer. Our hope for you is unshaken; for we know that as you share in our sufferings, you will also share in our consolation.[72]

---

[72] 2 Corinthians 1:3–7. The RSV's "comfort" has here been replaced by "consolation."

The logic of the passage is that neither affliction nor consolation are felt by individuals alone. Christ's sufferings and his encouragement are felt by all of us, and we in turn are all the better equipped to comfort/console those who are suffering. The true comfort, consolation, and encouragement stem ultimately from God himself.

Later in the same letter, Paul speaks to the vulnerability and complexity of life in the age we inhabit, and the polarities that result. "We are afflicted in every way, but not crushed; perplexed, but not driven to despair; persecuted, but not forsaken; struck down, but not destroyed."[73] The same kind of thinking returns later in the letter. The life of the Christian, or of anyone who is genuinely seeking to live in the truth and in a right way, is inevitably plagued by despair that can only be countered by faith and hope. Note the reference to sorrow amidst joy when Paul speaks of himself and his friends "as dying, and behold we live; as punished, and yet not killed; as sorrowful, yet always rejoicing; as poor, yet making many rich; as having nothing, and yet possessing everything."[74]

"Sorrowful, yet always rejoicing." Having enumerated this coincidence of opposites, Paul speaks of distress, identifying its different qualities: grief can be healthy, useless, or even damaging. "For godly grief produces a repentance that leads to salvation and brings no regret, but worldly grief produces death."[75] Context: Paul sent a difficult letter that evidently caused upset. But he is pleased, not because he enjoys causing grief but because the people acted on it, addressing their problems to become a better community. Paul's message is that sorrow, grief, is to be expected

[73] 2 Corinthians 4:8–9.
[74] 2 Corinthians 6:9–10.
[75] 2 Corinthians 7:10.

in this world. The problem arises when grief is allowed to fester, to destroy. One should beware, in other words, of neurotic grief, or, as we might diagnose it today, of attachment to guilt and regret, or of depression and other ailments.

Even as Paul invites his readers to discern different kinds and extents of desolation, we find a considerable tradition that distinguishes sorrow, compunction, and grief, from *despair*. "Despair" means a state beyond "extreme grief," namely the conviction that there is no hope for good. Within the tradition, despair is considered a grave error, even an offense against God. Despair is "ungodly grief" because it denies God's power, love, and salvation, however remote these might feel during extreme suffering. As is the case for silence, so with grief: sorrow, like silence, may engender something creative, something beautiful, something that will bear the traces of the sorrow whence it came.

The Desert and Monastic Tradition

The great writers of the monasteries and deserts of the Christian East—the Church calls them "Fathers" and "Mothers"—had a lot to say about bright sadness.[76] Perhaps more accurately, they wrote with particular depth about mourning and about watchfulness. The idea of joy, lightness, brightness was somehow taken as understood; to them, it did not need to be emphasized. Gladness was not absent from their writings, but other authors would fill in the blanks on how to rejoice in the Lord. These writers, who flourished from the fourth to the seventh centuries, and the

[76]A summary of texts and an introduction to their context may be found in William Harmless, *Desert Christians: An Introduction to the Literature of Early Monasticism* (Oxford: Oxford University Press, 2004).

monastics and hermits whose thinking they captured in their texts, served as guides for a life of maximal sobriety and self-vigilance, in a battle against pride, against gluttony for power and gratification. Their writings are not easy for many of us to understand or cozy up to. But their wisdom is enduring and finds purchase in Pärt's music.

One of the greatest of these luminaries is St John Climacus, whose writings have been staples of monastic and lay reading from the time of their writing in the seventh century up to the present day.[77] Climacus was highly influential on Arvo Pärt, notably during the pivotal 1970s. He has some significant observations on the nature of *mourning*, and Step 7 of his thirty-step *Ladder of Divine Ascent* is dedicated entirely to that theme. Like the rest of his text, this section is by no means absent of joy—he can speak of "cheerful renunciation"[78]—but it is grounded in the sensibility of compunction, repentance, and mourning.

He writes on these themes realizing that they require thoughtful reflection and are liable to be misapplied. We might take note today of the potential confusion between a genuine mournfulness about one's distance from God on the one hand, and a clinical depression on the other. The former is encouraged; the latter requires professional attention. Climacus also warned against affecting "false mourning," a kind of self-indulgent sadness, in order to demonstrate one's great piety to oneself and to others.

---

[77] All references will be taken from Colm Luibheid and Norman Russell, *John Climacus: The Ladder of Divine Ascent,* Classics of Western Spirituality (Mahwah, NJ: Paulist Press, 1982), see especially "Step 7," 136–145.
[78] Ibid., 136.

According to Climacus, mourning, correctly construed, is a vital instrument in the fashioning of a life in God. He speaks of mourning as something to be *pursued*. One must hold fast to it, and not let it be dissipated by noise, worldly care, luxury, and frivolity.[79] Yes, he writes of it as *joyful sorrow,* and holy compunction. But Climacus warns against mourning at one moment and going in for high living the next, against seeking a kind of oscillation between the two states: "It is like someone who pelts the dog of sensuality with bread. It looks as if he is driving him off when in fact he is actually encouraging the dog to stay by him."[80] Joyful sorrow is a simultaneous temperament. The two interpenetrate; they are interwoven. "Comfort is the balm of a distressed soul, which at the same time both cries and shouts happily, just like a child."[81]

Although the two are intermingled, there is a causal relationship. Proper mourning is liable to bring on a deep-set and enduring consolation, and even joy. "The one who wears blessed, God-given mourning like a wedding garment gets to know the spiritual laughter of the soul."[82] The tears we shed for our sins—i.e. our distance from God and from all that is true and right—are "cool waters of blessed sadness" that we must "guard like the apple of our eye" for "they have a power greater than anything that comes from our own efforts and our own meditation."[83] Their "power" is to bring the joy of consolation, as well as the more enduring and meaningful gift of a right relationship with God and with the world—*enlightenment.* "The depths of mourning have witnessed

[79]Ibid., 137.
[80]Ibid., 138.
[81]Ibid., 143.
[82]Ibid., 140.
[83]Ibid., 139.

comfort, and enlightenment has followed on purity of heart." Climacus is talking of true freedom and lightness of being, brought on through a right mourning:

> As I ponder the true nature of compunction, I find myself amazed by the way in which inward joy and gladness mingle with what we call mourning and grief, like honey in a comb. There must be a lesson here, and it surely is that compunction is properly a gift from God, so that there is a real pleasure in the soul, since God secretly brings consolation to those who in their heart of hearts are repentant.[84]

In pondering the configuration of sorrow and joy, Climacus would remind us that although a proper mourning is a deeply appropriate state of mind, "God does not demand or desire that someone should mourn out of sorrow of the heart, but rather that *out of love for Him he should rejoice with the laughter of the soul.*"[85] This means that however brightness and mourning are "configured," the root disposition, the motivation that guides everything, is the love of God.

St Silouan the Athonite

Silouan the Athonite (1866–1938) was to many of his contemporaries a simple Russian monk of the Monastery of St Panteleimon on the Holy Mountain of Athos. He is now more commonly regarded (especially throughout the Orthodox world) as one of the greatest spiritual luminaries to have emerged in modern times.

[84]Ibid., 141.
[85]P. 141, emphasis added.

In his life Silouan experienced grace and profound loss. His message is difficult to apprehend, as it is so hard for most of us to relate both to his intense nearness to God, and the depth of his struggles with his own perceived sinfulness. Yet, although at a considerable remove from these sharp polarities of height and depth, something of his words is capable of reaching us, or at least telling us something about the relationship between loss and hope, sweetness and grief. Silouan experienced gut-wrenching struggles with his own pride, a battle plagued by visions of demons. In the utter depths of that struggle, Christ himself gave him a phrase to live by, a word that would hold the key to his onward journey in God:

> Keep your mind in hell, and despair not.
> Держи ум твой во аде, и не отчаивайся.

This seems so distant from our postmodern age. Silouan's disciple, Father Sophrony, acknowledging how inaccessible these words may sound, explains that a person must see him/herself in hell, where the fires will consume his or her sinful passions—most particularly the passion of pride. This descent accompanies Christ's own descent into Hades from the cross. As such it is a descent into *humility*, into realizing "I am the least of persons, this is where I belong." There, the enemies of our soul cannot touch us since they cannot bear the ineffable humility of Christ. This is where we are to keep our minds. But the accompanying of Christ in his descent will, by grace, entail joining him too in the resurrection. As the Apostle Paul writes in his letter to the Romans, "For if we have been united with him in a death like his, we shall certainly be united with him in a resurrection like his."[86]

---

[86]Romans 6:5.

That the wider world has come to know Silouan at all, that after years of local veneration he came to be officially recognized as a saint, that he is now read and venerated with such love around the globe, owes to Father Sophrony (Sakharov), Silouan's spiritual son. Silouan bequeathed his writings to Sophrony, who reverently and lovingly published them while also telling the story of Silouan's life and examining his significance.[87] It was Father Sophrony who, in obedience to Silouan, left the Holy Mountain and founded a monastic community in Essex, England, that exists to this day. That community is near and dear to Arvo Pärt, who had begun to read about Silouan during his period of transition and came to enjoy a close relationship with Sophrony over many years, until the latter's death in 1993.

Pärt first began to try to translate Silouan's legacy into music during the 1980s, by composing a setting of his meditation "Adam's Lament." He worked on the project in consultation with Father Sophrony over several years, but became overwhelmed with the task and laid it aside. He took it up afresh more than two decades later with the more feasible goal of setting just a portion of the text. He completed it in 2010 and it premiered that same year in Istanbul. Before that, however, he composed *Silouan's Song* (1991),[88]

---

[87]See the monumental volume Sakharov, *Saint Silouan the Athonite*. The theology and message of St Silouan is explored still further in Archimandrite Zacharias, *The Enlargement of the Heart: "Be Ye Also Enlarged" (2 Corinthians 6:13) in the Theology of Saint Silouan the Athonite and Elder Sophrony of Essex* (South Canaan, PA: Mount Thabor Publishing, 2006). Father Sophrony authored several works on life in God, on asceticism, and on prayer. There is also a study of Sophrony's theology: Nicholas Sakharov, *I Love Therefore I Am: The Theological Legacy of Archimandrite Sophrony* (op. cit.).

[88]Its full title is *Silouan's Song. "My soul yearns after the Lord . . ."* and it is dedicated to Archimandrite Sophrony and his monastic community.

based on another of Silouan's prayers, although the words themselves are unsung:

> My soul yearns after the Lord and I seek Him in tears. How could I do other than seek Thee, for Thou first didst seek and find me, and gavest me to delight in Thy Holy Spirit, and my soul fell to loving Thee.
>
> Thou seest, O Lord, my grief and my tears . . . Hadst Thou not drawn me with Thy love, I could not seek Thee as I seek Thee now; but Thy spirit gave me to know Thee, and my soul rejoices that Thou art my God and my Lord, and I yearn after Thee even to tears.[89]

A preeminent theme in the writings of St Silouan concerns the soul's yearning for God, which is deeply linked in Orthodox thought to the kind of mourning we explored above through St John Climacus. In the case of Silouan, the disposition of yearning, seeking, striving, is made more poignant: he had intimately known the presence of God and experienced in his soul the Grace of the Holy Spirit, before losing them. The memory of them made their absence all the more excruciating for him.

Silouan meditates on Adam, the first-created: who is a better emblem of the contrast between closeness with God and alienation from him?[90] Adam, infused with God's breath/Spirit,[91]

[89]Sakharov, *Saint Silouan the Athonite*, 269.

[90]The theme of Adam's mourning for the loss of Paradise has been taken up in the hymnography of the Church: a Kontakion hymn, probably dating from the fifth century may be found at http://www.anastasis.org.uk/adam%27s_lament.htm (accessed November 19, 2014). The Sunday preceding Great Lent in the Orthodox Church is consecrated to the theme of The Expulsion of Adam and Eve from Paradise, and employs a rich hymnography.

[91]Genesis 2:7.

knew God, and his own spirit was "glad and at rest."[92] When Adam transgressed and was exiled from Paradise, his grief was unbounded and inconsolable:

> The Holy Spirit is love and sweetness for soul, mind, and body. And those who have come to know God by the Holy Spirit stretch upward day and night, insatiable, to the living God, for the love of God is exceeding sweet. But when the soul loses grace, her tears flow as she seeks the Holy Spirit anew.[93]

The text of the lament moves between a description of Adam, a dialogue between Adam and God, and a dialogue between Adam and the narrator—speaking now in his own person, and now as representative of all humanity. We learn of Adam's grief in his loss. We learn of the narrator's own loss, and that of all Adam's legacy, everyone who has lived and has yet to live. In these exchanges we learn that Adam's transgression brought shame, compunction, a godly mourning, and repentance. And we learn that God, in his love, has brought Adam to an even more beautiful paradise, in heaven with the Holy Trinity. Adam still recalls his feelings of bereavement, but only in order to counsel his children, who are still in this world, but these are now behind him: he exists in the joy and love of God.

This message given to St Silouan is an especially arresting iteration of bright sadness. As in the Psalms, Paul, John Climacus—as in Christ, really—it is emphatically a bright *sadness*. Rather than a state of bliss that bears a reminder of fallenness, it constitutes a state of sober, watchful mourning, unshakably faithful in God's

[92] "Adam's Lament," in Sakharov, *Saint Silouan the Athonite*, 448, and in Appendix III below.
[93] Ibid., 451.

love, Christ's self-emptying victory, and the Grace of the Holy
Spirit.

Bright Sadness in the Music of Arvo Pärt

A couple of years ago I told Pärt about listening to *Tabula Rasa*
with a friend who, as *Silentium* was drawing to its close, reacted
with these words: "It feels like he's saying, 'There's so much suffering and sadness in the world. But somehow everything's going
to be okay.'" Before even responding to me Arvo immediately
turned to his wife, Nora, reporting to her gleefully that another
person has "got it." As we saw earlier, he greets such reactions
with jubilation. Hearing them, he experiences the assurance of
being understood.

At the outset of this section I identified several metaphors that
have been applied to Arvo Pärt's music. Suffering and consolation, straying and stability, human and divine, sin and the forgiveness of sins. These share certain common qualities, primarily as
coincidences of opposites. The one element is always the more
vulnerable, broken. The other is somehow whole, and healing.
The question is, how does the composer interweave these characteristics into the music such that they are widely perceived? How
does he convey a subtle reality without resorting to more obvious
or cruder means such as manipulation of tempo, minor-major
tonal shifts, and the like?

An important part of the answer lies with *tintinnabuli*, the style,
the ethos, the world that Pärt has created, that space that he
"sometimes wanders into."[94] As we are about to see, *tintinnabuli*

[94]See Hillier, *Arvo Pärt*, 87.

is founded on a specific rule, at root a very simple one. Its basis in two voices—one melodic and one triadic—has direct bearing on the bright-sadness of the music. But the rule is not everything: the conveyance of complex and somehow opposing states of the human spirit relies on other factors as well. This is to say that the mystery lies in the *application* of the principle, and therefore ultimately with the composer himself. What's more, the same joyful sorrow is conveyed in works whose adherence to the rule is either looser or non-existent—so the rule, though significant, is not the single hidden key. But it is a crucial one.

Two critics are especially significant in explicating *tintinnabuli*. One is Paul Hillier, who explained it in a manner and with a terminology that subsequent Pärt musicologists have all drawn upon.[95] The other is Leopold Brauneiss, who has built on Hillier's foundations to construct several deep-structure analyses.[96] For the purposes of the present study, I will set out the basic principle, initially by means of telling the story of its genesis.

The Second Voice

If we go back to 1968, we can revisit the brilliant but tortured composition, *Credo,* and the years-long silence that followed. Pärt's search for how to speak again with music involved a search for purity, unity, simplicity. In that odyssey, the role of early music and especially Gregorian chant (NB: *monophonic* chant) was inestimable. He focused his musical pursuit entirely

[95] Ibid., 86–97.
[96] Among several essays, see especially Leopold Brauneiss, "Tintinnabuli: An Introduction," in Restagno, 107–162, and "Musical Archetypes: The Basic Elements of the Tintinnabuli Style," in *Cambridge Companion*, 49–75.

on monophony, filling hundreds of notebooks with melodies. He would read a psalm, and write a melody. He would observe a shape, and write a melody. He set the words of the Psalms and the Jesus Prayer to melodies: just notes, free of time-signatures and measures.[97] These were like a stream of water, often beautiful—Pärt's gift for melody has always been enormous—but leading nowhere in particular.

Over the years from 1968–1976, despite the transitional *Symphony No. 3*, a creative block weighed increasingly on his life. And then, something happened. We know the day and time that it happened. Nora tells the story:

> It was the seventh of February 1976. And I was going to go out with a pram with Immanuel, because it was the first sun and the birds were singing. And Arvo says to me, 'Wait! Don't go anywhere.' And that was when *Alina* was born. The moment of birth during that day was the *discovery of the second voice*. And so for us this was the "Big Bang" of creation.[98]

Arvo adds: "And the second voice is . . . 'Without me, you can do nothing.' Nothing."[99]

---

[97]In the documentary by Dorian Supin, *24 Preludes for a Fugue*, we can hear Pärt discuss and play a melody he wrote to the Jesus Prayer, from 40:05. A page from those notebooks with the Jesus Prayer is reproduced here in color insert.

[98]Bouteneff, Recorded Interview with Arvo and Nora Pärt (op. cit.). Note that in the documentary film *24 Preludes for a Fugue* the year of this discovery, and *Alina's* composition, is given as 1975, since that is the year written on the notebook. But Pärt confirms that the year in fact was 1976.

[99]Ibid. He is quoting Jesus's words in John 15:5—words that he has set to music in *I Am the True Vine* (1996).

What is this "second voice?" It is the voice of the triad. As in, do, mi, sol. La, re, fa. The notes of a major or minor triad, struck simultaneously, would form a chord that might ground a melody. There is a physical/acoustical explanation for the function of the triad, resting in the overtone series that resonates in a note's octave, fifth, and (major) third. The triad will acoustically underscore a melody's tonal center. The meeting of melody and triad is in itself nothing new. Why, then, did "the discovery of the second voice" strike Pärt as a "Big Bang?"

It must have had something to do with the configuration of the voices. Pärt had obviously known that a melody could consist in any series of notes. Now, what if each of those melodic notes were accompanied by a voice with a strictly limited tone set? The basic, distilled, and fundamental tone set that is the triad—positions 1, 3, and 5 in a diatonic scale? Suddenly, you have a Melody (M-voice) + Triad (T-voice).[100]

The result is at once a primal principle, located in elementary music and acoustical theory, as well as something completely fresh. The newness and the familiarity alike can be illustrated by way of two of Pärt's earliest and most-heard *tintinnabuli* compositions that are also among his seemingly simplest: *Für Alina* (1976) and *Spiegel im Spiegel* (1978). The first notes we hear in *Spiegel im Spiegel* are the triad, repeated over and over.[101] Then the melody instrument enters, proceeding one step or half-step at a time, as the T voice keeps playing the relative triad, in one

---

[100]The "M" and "T" designations (T is for triad and also for *tintinnabuli*) are Paul Hillier's—see *Arvo Pärt,* 93ff.

[101]These triads seem directly to echo Bach's *Prelude in C,* so central to Pärt's earlier works.

inversion or another, with bell-like punctuations played far above or far below the melody register.

Spiegel is illustrative because the triad is so obvious. But *Alina* is still more indicative of the *tintinnabuli* principle: the two voices, M and T, two piano keys, are always struck simultaneously, showing us that they cannot possibly exist separately from each other. Each "note-event" is in fact a pair of notes, a pair that conspires to evoke a single whole. Pärt and his commentators frequently illustrate the phenomenon with the paradoxical equation, "$1+1=1$." The two notes together constitute a unity that, strangely, could not have existed if the notes were in isolation. Sounded together, it is indeed as if we are listening to the voices of the eponymous little bells.[102]

Through Pärt's *tintinnabuli* compositions, the pairing of melody with triad works in a myriad of ways and settings, across different tempos and tonalities, in simple as well as lush and complex applications. In some pieces the M and T voices are simultaneous (e.g., *Passio*), in others they are staggered (e.g., *My Heart's in the Highlands*), in others they are lodged within more complex polyphony. *Tintinnabuli* undergirds the simplicity of the *Missa Syllabica* (1977), and in a completely different way it undergirds the huge chordal structures of *In Principio* (2003).

Other Factors

The nature of the *tintinnabuli* style is such that Pärt's compositions are often easy to recognize. Yet they are also extremely varied. The diverse results stem from the different applications of the rule, for example in different degrees of exactitude: very strictly,

---

[102]The score may be seen in Hillier, *Arvo Pärt*, 88–89.

as in *Passio*, and sometimes loosely, as in *Wallfahrtslied*. It can be applied within major tonalities, as in the "Credo" of the *Berliner Messe*, and minor tonalities, as in most of his music—Pärt emphatically tends toward the minor.

Furthermore the basic M-voice+T-voice principle co-exists with other techniques and rules. We saw earlier on how melodies are shaped and punctuated in specific ways by the texts that underlie them. Melodies and chords are also shaped according to principles of addition, mirroring, and multiplication techniques that have been explored in some detail by Brauneiss.[103]

Then there are specific rules that apply to particular compositions. For example, in the early *tintinnabuli* works *Cantus, Fratres, Arbos*, all from 1977, the melodies and rhythms unfold according to clear patterns. The melody of *Cantus* consists simply in a descending A-minor (Aeolian or natural minor) scale, played in five different tempos by the different string sections; like *Arbos*, it is a mensuration canon (a melody is introduced and then reproduced by different voices and possibly in different tempos). Numerous musicologists and mathematicians have analyzed and diagrammed Pärt's compositions, publishing them in books and essays as well as on the Internet so that all may see their visual beauty.[104] As part of his composition process, Pärt makes diagrams, sometimes very simple ones, that depict on the metaphorical level how the composition will flow.[105]

[103]See Brauneiss, "Musical Archetypes", esp. 53–55, and also his "Tintinnabuli: An Introduction" esp. 126–138.

[104]The Wikipedia page for *Cantus* currently features a clear analysis of that piece. A useful exploration of *Fratres* may be found here: www.linusakesson.net/music/fratres/index.php.

[105]Many of these may be found scattered throughout the Arvo Pärt Centre publication *In Principio: The Word in Arvo Pärt's Music* (op. cit.).

Pärt typically takes great care to formulate the structure and rules of a composition before he writes the music itself. We have already observed some of the rules related to text: how the shape and syllables of the text will dictate a composition's melodic and rhythmic form. Such principles aggregate with others: the broader diagrams that serve as musical blueprints, the ways in which melodies and voices aggregate and reduce, and the fundamental rule of the interaction of M and T voices. Once Pärt has established all of the principles, a considerable part of the composition process consists in "simply" following the rules—and sometimes breaking them.

Structure, discipline, and obedience—these words by themselves may sound like either a totalitarian nightmare or part of a healthy and genuine spiritual life. Technically, they can be either. But spiritual adepts of many traditions and none, and artists of all kinds often recognize the basis of genuine freedom in regulation, renunciation, and obedience. Brauneiss interprets Pärt's attitude toward rules in similar terms: "The belief that a restraining of the ego, enabling it to accept outside forces, will lead to self-perfection, is ultimately a religious attitude."[106] So much so that his disposition of submission, says Brauneiss, plays at least as great a role in the religious character of Pärt's compositions as do their sacred texts and other evident features.

He is right. Both the creation of the formulae and the adherence to their rules are a matter of discernment, discipline, and humility, exercised in freedom. The obedience is not slavish, but creative. To illustrate, there is almost no rule that Pärt has established for a composition that he has not broken within the same

---

[106]Brauneiss, "Tintinnabuli: An Introduction," 125.

composition. *Alina,* as we saw, is based on a T and an M voice struck simultaneously. Furthermore, the T voice will be the closest possible triad note below the M voice. Once the M voice is written, therefore, the T voice writes itself—except for one note that is foreign to the B-minor triad: a C#. That "illegal" note's contribution to the composition, its structure and feel, is impossible to overstate. It is the exception that not only proves the rule, but defies it so that the piece may sing. To underscore its gentle but significant role, every proper reproduction of this piece's score features a small flower under that C#.

The Interwoven Polarities

Tintinnabuli's two-voice principle of one sound made of two plays a primary role in configuring and conveying the bright sadness of Pärt's music. Recall the various metaphors that critics have used to describe the effect of his compositions—straying and stable, vulnerable and dispassionate, suffering and consoling, human and divine. The M and T voices are a vital instrument for the expression of these dualities. Generally speaking, the M-voice, the melody, evokes the human vulnerability and suffering, and the T-voice evokes the divine stability and redemption.

That underlying logic of *tintinnabuli* came into focus almost as soon as the second voice came to Pärt's consciousness, practically together with the birth of *tintinnabuli*. The very year of the first works composed in that style (1976) a concert of Pärt works, called "Tintinnabuli," was performed by the ensemble Hortus Musicus. Pärt's preparatory notes for that concert already identified the fundamental affective principle: "Each phrase breathes alone. Its inner pain and the solace of that pain make up its breathing when they are inextricably linked together."[107]

The respective characters of the two voices are lodged within basic musical principles, especially in the nature and function of the triad. The cosmological structural basis in the triangle, the Trinitarian understanding of God, the narrative rule of three, all can be seen as musically reflected in the diatonic scale, grounded in the triad as a matter of acoustics. The triad is the skeleton on which the scale is hung. And so the triad voice tends to function in terms of stability, grounding the forays of the melody voice.

The straying melody and the stable triad make for a legitimately useful image for what is going on in the music, even if it would be too simplistic to insist exclusively on the one-to-one equation of the voice and its affective function: melody = human suffering, and triad = divine consolation. The net result of the coincidence of voices is indisputable: *it is the relationship of tension and resolution.* Put a triad voice and a melody voice together and the resulting intervals will alternate in consonance and dissonance. In listening to *Alina,* you will hear, from the very outset of the piece, major and minor seconds, thirds, and some fourths, though separated by an octave. Tension, resolution, tension, resolution-resolution.

Tintinnabuli in Theology: 1+1=1

Tension, resolution. It sounds too simple to carry any meaningful content. But the configuration of the suffering and the consolation

---

[107]Program notes © Arvo Pärt Centre, published in Russian and in English translation in *Music and Literature* 1 (Fall 2012), 20–21.

in the music makes for the "heart-rending union" of voices and sensibilities. The tension and resolution of *tintinnabuli* are created not primarily by the timbres of instruments, but at the level of the *notes*. The diverse orchestrations of the early *tintinnabuli* pieces is almost uncanny: *Fratres* has no fewer than eighteen official versions and *Summa* has ten. A later work, *Da Pacem Domine*, was composed in 2004 without fixed instrumentation, and eight more official versions emerged between 2006 and 2010. The orchestrations are not arbitrary—timbral considerations are still relevant—but the notes, triad and melody, are the primary actors.

The tension and the resolution at any given moment are created by the confluence of the stable and the straying, the divine and the human. To move back into a theological perspective, the divine-human relationship, in all its dimensions, is one of consonance and dissonance: divine and human are both radically other (*uncreated* versus *created*), and also intrinsically related (the one is made in the image of the other). Construing the voices as "divine and human" will speak also to the paradox of the eternal and the engaged, the tension of time and timelessness.[108] Contrary to the criticism of Pärt's music as sitting coldly outside of time, it is deeply embedded within it in solidarity with those who experience the vicissitudes of history. That is the melody. But it suggests timelessness in a way that both grounds the historical and indicates its upward movement. That is the triad.

Theology can provide some insights about how the two voices work together interdependently. On the one hand, one might assume, from a "reductive" sensibility, that nothing could be simpler than monophony, a melody on its own. Harmony or

---

[108]See above at pp. 35–37.

dissonance would seem to mar that purity. However, when the notes come together, even in "dissonance," they can seem mysteriously even *more* pure. That phenomenon is a demonstration of the paradoxical equation, $1+1=1$.

Pärt has elaborated on the *tintinnabuli* concept with yet another numerical illustration, the zeroes and ones of the digital binary:

> I am zero, and God is one. . . . "Zero" is what a person can produce, as a melodic line . . . and "one" is the other line. The *tintinnabuli* line. It makes the zero into something else than zero. . . . The triadic line is—these are lofty words—but it is like the "blessing" of the other line.[109]

The 0–1 concept is in some ways more theologically amenable because it retains the asymmetry of the divine-human relationship. God and humanity are not coequal and codependent partners; they are not "1"+"1." Genuine, uncontingent existence is only found on the divine side. Need, or contingency characterizes the human side. We need God in order to exist, and all the more so to be beautiful or good, while God technically has no need of us for his own existence. Yet, his love leads him to *choose* to exist together with us in something approaching a "mutually" completing way. What we have, therefore, is *symmetry-by-grace*: we are zero and God is one. But, by virtue of God's love, we are $1+1 = 1$.

Christ and the Trinity: More Confounding Arithmetic

The odd math that produces the equation above is nothing foreign to the Christian theologian, who is accustomed to the bending or wholesale repurposing of numerical logic. The two great

---

[109]Bouteneff, Recorded Interview with Arvo and Nora Pärt (op. cit.).

conundrums of Christian theology are effectively mathematical ones:

(a) how is it that a Trinity of persons (Father, Son, and Holy Spirit) is not in fact three deities, but a single God? How is it that three are one and one is three ($1+1+1=1$!)

(b) how is it that Jesus Christ, who is one person, can encompass two complete modes of being, divine and human? How can his two natures make up one person, such that $1+1=1$?

A full theological response to these conundrums took the better part of a millennium to address and is still a matter of interdenominational debate. I can only summarize the treatment of these questions in the Orthodox Church so that they might help in understanding the *tintinnabuli* equation and its music. As I keep saying, this is not to claim that Pärt evolved his system in a conscious relationship with these technical aspects of Orthodox Christian theology, it is only to suggest that Orthodox Christianity can shed light on Pärt's work.[110]

In the theological equations above as well as in the *tintinnabuli* formula, there are multiple "1's" on the left side, and a single "1" on the right side. What is it about the plural "1's" that they can constitute a single "1," rather than aggregate to a higher number? What is it about that single "1" that, despite evidently being a kind of composite, is not fragmented but retains or even *gains* integrity?

[110]Not dissimilarly, Brauneiss suggests that the writings of that fifteenth-century philosopher Nicolas of Cusa could yield insights into the principles of *tintinnabuli*, even as he notes at the outset that Pärt had never read Cusa (Leopold Brauneiss, "The Unification of Opposites: The Tintinnabuli Style in the Light of the Philosophy of Nicolaus Cusanus," *Music and Literature* 1, no. 1 (2012).

Let us first consider the Trinity: 1+1+1=1. The theological principles that enable this equation, as expressed within the Orthodox Christian tradition, run as follows:[111]

- There is one God, whom the Bible identifies as "The Father."
- The Father has with himself, from all eternity, a Son, and a Spirit.
  - o The Father does not and cannot exist without his Son and Spirit.
  - o The Son and the Spirit, each proceeding from the Father, fully share his nature, essence, and attributes; all three therefore are fully divine.
  - o That nature is perfectly simple: the three are not separated by time, location, temperament, volition. As such, they are *one*.

The upshot of these principles is that the unity of God is located with the person of the Father. But the Son and Spirit do not compromise divine unity; they actually *constitute* it. He is not God without them; they are not God without him. The plurality makes the unity.

We might relate this to *tintinnabuli* in that the addition of the second voice, which would logically seem to add complexity and numerical plurality, in fact constitutes a single whole. The resulting "1" is neither whole nor even truly existing without the unity of the two "1"s."

---

[111]A useful summary may be found in Thomas Hopko, "The Trinity in the Cappadocians," in *Christian Spirituality: Origins to the Twelfth Century*, ed. Bernard McGinn and John Meyendorff (New York: Crossroad, 1987).

Now let us consider Jesus Christ. He is, from all eternity, the Son of the Father, which means he is of the same nature or essence as the divine Father. He is also the son of Mary, which means he is of the same nature or essence as us human beings. Two different natures, two different categories of being—divine and human—co-existing in one person. $1+1=1$.

Here too, Orthodox Christian theology posits a mutual necessity between both sides of the equation. Jesus Christ has to be one person: if he is truly the savior of the world, the two natures, human and divine, cannot result in a hybrid creature resembling a minotaur (half-God half-man), or two separate persons, or the two "selves" of a multiple personality disorder. No—he is a single, integrated person. The Savior cannot be a mere human being, nor can he be only divine, simply pretending to be human. He has to be fully divine *and* fully human, the impassible and all-powerful one who also reaches the depths of human need and vulnerability.[112]

Orthodox theology expresses the union of the two natures, divine and human ($1+1$) by saying that the two are perfectly united, in that single person ($=1$). Since the Theological Definition of the Council of Chalcedon (451 CE), their unity has been specified carefully and precisely as:

- unconfused—the two natures do not fuse into an indistinguishable lump
- unchanged—the two natures completely retain their character as divine and as human

---

[112]See Peter C. Bouteneff, "Christ and Salvation," in *The Cambridge Companion to Orthodox Christian Theology*, ed. Mary B. Cunningham and Elizabeth Theokritoff (Cambridge: Cambridge University Press, 2008), 93–106.

- undivided—the two natures are always considered together
- unseparated—the two natures are never apart from each other.[113]

"Unconfused" and "unchanged" refer to the fact that the two voices retain their identities. They do not stop being distinct. You can recognize them, you can sing each of them. "Undivided" and "unseparated" refer to the absolute union that is formed of the two. Yes, you could sing each voice separately, but it is only when they are together that you have an integrated whole. Two voices, but one true sound.

These same adjectives could be applied by analogy to the union of the two *tintinnabuli* voices, with some important qualifications: Pärt speaks of the human voice as straying/sinning and the divine as stable/forgiving of sins. Christ's human "nature" never commits any sin, even as it retains its vulnerability and mortality. Also, we have already observed that the divine human relationship, in creation as in Christ, is not technically symmetrical. The interdependence of the human and the divine is an unbalanced one. Humanity is completely contingent upon God for its very existence; God does not similarly need humanity. In Christ as in creation, the "necessity" of the divine-human union is *chosen*, it is freely willed. God can exist completely on his own, but out of sheer love he chooses to be "made complete" through an indissoluble bond with humanity.

The theological bases and analogies for *tintinnabuli* are imperfect in another way as well: triads cannot stand alone as well as melodies can—something that, if applied to the divine-human

---

[113]These four qualifiers have figured into theological definitions ever since, even by churches who do not subscribe to the authority of that council.

relationship would reverse the dependencies. The stable "triad" voice that represents the divine stands at the basis of every note, as we see in the overtone series. Yet those three notes cannot by themselves create beautiful music. If anything, it is the monophonic melody that is capable of making sustained musical statements (think Gregorian chant; Bach's Cello Suites).

Beyond the Two Voices

The confluence of M and T voices is the primary feature of *tintinnabuli*. However, over time and with the aggregation of a larger body of compositions, *tintinnabuli* has come to mean more than the melody and the triad. We have seen how several principles are overlaid upon the basic M-T rule. Above and beyond even these structural blueprints we notice other characteristics of *tintinnabuli* compositions. Although there are notable exceptions, these include:[114]

- A purposeful reduction to essentials: melodically, harmonically (largely through the two-voice rubric, but also through the near absence of modulation), and rhythmically.
- A tendency toward slower tempos, where these essentials may carry their effect, where each note is given the opportunity to sound—such that "every blade of grass is given the status of a flower"[115]
- A tendency toward the minor key. It is possible to suggest that the *tintinnabuli* voices happen to sound better, that the tension-resolution dynamic works better, in the minor tonality.[116]

[114]See also Brauneiss, "Tintinnabuli: An Introduction," 109.
[115]In Supin, *24 Preludes for a Fugue*, at 12:40.
[116]Some compositions, such as *Te Deum* (1985) and *Berliner Messe* (1990), make stunning use of the interplay between major and minor keys.

These and other characteristics stem not from the rules but from the composer, his sensibilities, the personal, musical, and spiritual path he has trodden. The compositional rules and their deployment are two different things; both emanate from the composer. Others have attempted composing *tintinnabuli* works; people have even created computer algorithms—you can find them online—that churn out *tintinnabuli* music. Their results are deeply mixed and further support the mutual relationship of the principle and its application: the formula by itself is essentially neutral, capable of producing both profundity and pap.

What about the composer by himself, without the rule? I asked Pärt whether and how the "bright-sadness" ethos also informs the compositions that do not adhere to the *tintinnabuli* principle, or adhere to it more loosely. He replied, "Yes, it does. Of course! I can wear a different suit, but inside it's me. The suit doesn't change that. One suit is more 'suitable,' and perhaps inspires less perplexity. Maybe I also suffer in one suit more than another."[117]

Pärt tends toward the minor key. His music is frequently called "sad." Whatever we may have noted about *tintinnabuli* "sounding better" in the minor-key tonalities—something about the nature of the tension of the minor as against the built-in major of the overtone series, perhaps—the tonality comes from his sensibility. He resonates most deeply with that powerful, dominant strain of ancient Christian tradition that—even as it knows well the joy and lightness inherent in God's creation—keeps its head down. It is the same sensibility that gives rise to the psalms, the gospels, the desert teachings, and the writings of St Silouan. It is the heart that wearies in yearning for the Lord, the soul that awaits the Lord and

---

[117]Bouteneff, Recorded Interview with Arvo and Nora Pärt.

thirsts for him, the one that knows the depths to which humanity has sunk in its forgetting of God and of the world's genuine holiness. It is the soul that, from these very depths, will also never lose sight of the final redeeming power of the God of love.

* * *

Conclusio

To bring together many of the observations made in this book, I suggest a journey through Pärt's *Passio*. A setting of St John's Passion that works both within and outside established conventions of the genre, it was also Pärt's biggest, most ambitious composition by the time it appeared in 1982. This work set his career on a new trajectory, taking critics and listeners by storm, inspiring several stirring, insightful essays on this work as befitting a landmark in twentieth-century music.

The composition opens with an *exordium*, announcing what we are to hear: "The Passion of our Lord Jesus Christ according to John." Musically it is a majestic but sorrowful descent in half-note chords. It follows a descending A-minor scale, over an E pedal, and ends on a dissonant sub-dominant, one step short of bringing the scale to its concluding note. In plainer language, the introduction seems to take us down a staircase one step at a time, leaving us one step from the bottom. We have been escorted into the theater of the fallen world, seated just above its unfolding drama.

From this vantage we will spend the next hour following a familiar, grim series of events. Here, the music will never once leave the sad tonality of A-minor. The music is set up for maximum comprehensibility of the Latin text: it follows the rhythms of the words and phrases; it assigns each character a distinct musical identity. In this, the music is not neutral. It casts a quite different light, for example, on Pilate than on Jesus. Jesus, a bass, moves at a stately, measured pace over a narrow range, usually in whole and half steps. Pilate, a tenor, follows jagged, unstable intervals, including the tritone.

The narration is unhurried. Each event is accorded its full import. It is an extremely sober telling of the story, but a beautiful one. The composition adheres strictly to *tintinnabuli* rules: between the singers, instruments, and organ, the melody and triad voices are always accounted for, always ringing simultaneously. There is tension and resolution—gleanings of the bright within the sad. It is punctuated throughout with significant silences that are a part of the pacing, serving as the composition's inner breath. The music adheres to the text rules as well, but in interesting moments, those principles are broken to create dramatic effect: for example, Jesus's words from the cross, such as *Sitio* (I thirst) are significantly drawn out to command attention. His final words follow another slow, solemn musical descent, from E to the final, tonic A: *Consummatum est*. It is finished. The voices that comprise the evangelist-narrator announce his death in stark unison.

The silence that follows is somehow full, replete with the sorrow of the moment and with expectation. The mind is in hell, but not in despair. The *Passio* truncates the narration before the resurrection, ending once Christ has yielded up his spirit. But that leads into the piece's *conclusio*: a plea for Christ, who suffered for us, to have mercy on us. But lest we think of asking for mercy solely in terms of pathos, it is also a form of praise, an acknowledgment of God's power and a profession of trust in his love. Musically, it is in a new key: we are suddenly in D major. We realize that the entire hour-long composition was like a single chord that was awaiting its proper resolution. D major is what we have been waiting for, and at the same time it is where we have somehow been all along. Time and eternity are brought together; their tension is exposed even as it is resolved.

The conclusion includes its own significant descent, in the organ's bass pedals, following a downward D major scale. But that descent serves as the foundation for the choir's ascent, word-by-word. Unlike the *Exordium's* seven-step inconclusiveness, the eight words of the *conclusio* permit a resolution, in the final "Amen," that is stunningly sublime.

Theologically speaking, we have been drawn into heaven, although as we enter we know well that we could not have come here without having gone through hell. Nor could we have come here without the loving descent of God. Although the *Passio* story never arrives at the resurrection, the victory is won: not by the miracle of Jesus's resurrection, but precisely by his *death*. The death of the Divine Son represents the completion of God's entry into the world. All is now filled with God. The True Light has entered every place that was ever dark, among the living and among the dead, "and the darkness did not overcome it."[118] So, as bright/sad as things are in this strange interim time we live in, all is in fact accomplished. *Consummatum est*. And what lies ahead is an ever-renewing brightness.

---

[118]John 1:5.

APPENDICES

I. Authorized Chronological List of Arvo Pärt's Compositions[1]

- 1956–1957 Four Easy Dances for Piano. Music for children's theatre
  1. Puss in Boots / Saabastega kass
  2. Little Red Riding Hood and the Wolf / Punamütsike ja hunt
  3. Butterflies / Liblikad
  4. Dance of the Ducklings / Pardipoegade tants
- 1956–1960 Five Children's Songs [for children's choir (unisono) and piano]
  1. I Am Already Big / Mina olen juba suur

[1]Reproduced by permission of the Arvo Pärt Centre, who add the following notes:
- The chronological list is based on the dates of the original versions of the works, i.e, in their original instrumentation. The dates of their completion and of revision(s) are separated by a slash. Only the most recent version is valid.
- The new arrangements are listed chronologically immediately below the original version of the work. Usually they share the same title, but there are exceptions, as in the case of *In spe* and *An den Wassern* . . .
- The title and the subtitle are separated by a full stop.
- As to the titles, the slash also separates the work's international title (usually as published) and its original title (corresponding to the composer's manuscript). These double titles are used mainly for presenting earlier works (composed before 1980).

2. Firefly's Song / Jaaniussi laul

3. Frogs / Konnad

4. Ladybird's Song / Lepatriinu laul

5. The Doll Has No Name / Nukul pole nime

- 1958 Partita for Piano
- 1958–1959 Two Sonatinas for Piano
  - 1958 Sonatina for Piano No. 1
  - 1959 Sonatina for Piano No. 2
- 1959 Our Garden / Meie aed [cantata for children's choir and orchestra]
- 1960 Nekrolog / Nekroloog [for orchestra]
- 1962 Let the Snow Swish / Las vihistab [for children's choir (unisono) and piano; published also with Estonian title "Näärilaul"]
- 1962 Father Frost / Näärivana [for children's choir (unisono) and piano]
- 1963 Symphony No. 1 "Polyphonic" [for orchestra]
- 1963 Perpetuum mobile [for orchestra]
- 1963 Solfeggio / Solfedžo [for mixed choir a cappella]
  - 2002 Solfeggio / Solfedžo [for saxophone quartet]
  - 2008 Solfeggio / Solfedžo [for string quartet]
  - 2010 Solfeggio / Solfedžo [for 8 or 4 violoncellos]
- 1964 Collage über B-A-C-H / Kollaaž teemal B-A-C-H [for strings, oboe, harpsichord and piano]
  - 1994 Concerto piccolo über B-A-C-H [for solo trumpet, strings, harpsichord and piano]
- 1964 Diagramme / Diagrammid [for piano]
- 1964 Quintettino [for flute, oboe, clarinet, bassoon and horn]
- 1966 Pro et contra [concerto for violoncello and orchestra]
- 1966 Symphony No. 2 [for orchestra]

- 1968 Credo [for mixed choir, piano and orchestra]
- 1971 Symphony No. 3 [for orchestra]
- 1973/2010 Ukuaru Waltz / Ukuaru valss [for piano]
- 1976/1989 Sarah Was Ninety Years Old / Saara oli 90-aastane
  [for 3 voices STT, percussion and organ]
- 1976 In spe [for voices SATB and any selection of instruments]
  - 1984/1991 An den Wassern zu Babel saßen wir und weinten.
  Psalm 137 [for soloists or choir SATB and organ]
  - 1995 An den Wassern zu Babel . . . Psalm 137 [for trombone
    and chamber orchestra]
  - 1996 An den Wassern zu Babel . . . Psalm 137 [for soloists
    SATB and instruments]
  - 2010 In spe [for wind quintet and string orchestra]
- 1976 Für Alina / Aliinale [for piano]
- 1976 Pari intervallo [four-part music, without fixed
    instrumentation]
  - 1980 Pari intervallo [for organ]
  - 1980 Pari intervallo [for 4 recorders]
  - 1995 Pari intervallo [for clarinet, trombone and string
    orchestra]
  - 2002 Pari intervallo [for saxophone quartet]
  - 2008 Pari intervallo [for four-hand piano or 2 pianos]
  - 2010 Pari intervallo [for 8 or 4 violoncellos]
- 1976 Trivium [for organ]
- 1976/2001 Wenn Bach Bienen gezüchtet hätte . . . / Kui Bach
    oleks mesilasi pidanud . . . [for piano, wind quintet,
    string orchestra and percussion]
- 1977 Arbos [for (early music) instruments, without fixed
    instrumentation]
  - 1977 Arbos [for 7 (8) recorders and 3 triangles ad lib.]

- 1986/2001 Arbos [for 8 brass instruments and percussion]
- 1977/1996 Cantate Domino canticum novum. Psalm 95 [for mixed choir and soloists SATB and organ]
- 1977/1980 Cantus in Memory of Benjamin Britten / Cantus Benjamin Britteni mälestuseks [for string orchestra and a bell]
- 1977 Fratres. Three-part music [without fixed instrumentation]
  - 1982 Fratres. Three-part music [for 4, 8, 12 . . . violoncellos]
  - 1983/1991 Fratres. Three-part music [for string orchestra and percussion]
  - 1985/1989 Fratres. Three-part music [for string quartet]
  - 1990 Fratres. Three-part music [for wind octet and percussion]
  - 2004 Fratres. Three-part music [for wind orchestra]
  - 2007 Fratres. Three-part music [for chamber ensemble]
  - 2009 Fratres. Three-part music [for 3 recorders, percussion and violoncello or viola da gamba]
  - 1980 Fratres. Three-part music with solo-variations [for violin and piano]
  - 1989 Fratres. Three-part music with solo-variations [for violoncello and piano]
  - 1992 Fratres. Three-part music with solo-variations [for violin, string orchestra and percussion]
  - 1993 Fratres. Three-part music with solo-variations [for trombone, string orchestra and percussion]
  - 1995 Fratres. Three-part music with solo-variations [for violoncello, string orchestra and percussion]
  - 2000 Fratres. Three-part music with solo-variations [for guitar, string orchestra and percussion]
  - 2002 Fratres. Three-part music with solo-variations [for saxophone quartet]

- 2003 Fratres. Three-part music with solo-variations [for viola and piano]
- 2006 Fratres. Three-part music with solo-variations [for 4 percussion players]
- 2008 Fratres. Three-part music with solo-variations [for viola, string orchestra and percussion]

• 1977/1996 Missa syllabica [for mixed choir a cappella]
  - 1977 Missa syllabica [for soloists SATB and chamber ensemble]
  - 1996 Missa syllabica [for mixed choir and organ]
  - 2009 Missa syllabica [for soloists SATB and string quartet]

• 1977 Summa [for mixed choir or soloists SATB a cappella]
  - 1990 Summa [for violins, 2 violas and violoncello]
  - 1991 Summa [for string orchestra]
  - 1991 Summa [for string quartet]
  - 2002/2009 Summa [for saxophone quartet]
  - 2005 Summa [for recorder quartet]
  - 2008 Summa [for trombone quartet]
  - 2010 Summa [for guitar quartet]
  - 2010 Summa [for 8 or 4 violoncellos]
  - 2011 Summa [for 2 guitars]

• 1977 Tabula rasa [for 2 violins, prepared piano and string orchestra]
  - 1977 Tabula rasa [for violin, viola, prepared piano and string orchestra]

• 1977 Variations for the Healing of Arinushka / Variatsii na vyzdorovlenie Arinushki / Variatsioonid Ariinuska tervekssaamise puhul [for piano]

• 1978 Spiegel im Spiegel / Peegel peeglis [for violin and piano]
  - 1978 Spiegel im Spiegel / Peegel peeglis [for viola and piano]
  - 1978 Spiegel im Spiegel / Peegel peeglis [for violoncello and piano]

- 2003 Spiegel im Spiegel / Peegel peeglis [for clarinet or bass clarinet and piano]
- 2003 Spiegel im Spiegel / Peegel peeglis [for horn and piano]
- 2005 Spiegel im Spiegel / Peegel peeglis [for alto flute and piano]
- 2005 Spiegel im Spiegel / Peegel peeglis [for oboe and piano]
- 2006 Spiegel im Spiegel / Peegel peeglis [for contrabass and piano]
- 2006 Spiegel im Spiegel / Peegel peeglis [for cor anglais and piano]
- 2009 Spiegel im Spiegel / Peegel peeglis [for bassoon and piano]
- 2010 Spiegel im Spiegel / Peegel peeglis [for organ]
- 1980 Annum per annum [for organ]
- 1980 De profundis. Psalm 130 (129) [for male choir TTBB, percussion ad lib. and organ]
  - 2008 De profundis. Psalm 130 (129) [for male choir TTBB and chamber orchestra]
- 1982 Passio Domini Nostri Jesu Christi secundum Joannem [for soloists, mixed choir, instrumental quartet and organ]
- 1984 Es sang vor langen Jahren. Motette für de la Motte [for alto or countertenor, violin and viola]
- 1984/2004 Hymn to a Great City [for 2 pianos]
- 1984 Ein Wallfahrtslied / Pilgrims' Song. Psalm 121 (120) [for tenor or baritone and string quartet]
  - 2001 Ein Wallfahrtslied / Pilgrims' Song. Psalm 121 (120) [for male choir TB and string orchestra]
- 1984/1997 Zwei slawische Psalmen. Psalm 117, Psalm 131 [for mixed choir or soloists SACtTB a cappella]
- 1985/1991 Psalom [for string quartet]
  - 1995 Psalom [for string orchestra]
  - 2010 Psalom [for 8 or 4 violoncellos]

- 1985 Stabat Mater [for soprano, countertenor or alto, tenor, violin, viola and violoncello]
  - 2008 Stabat Mater [for choir SAT and string orchestra]
- 1985/1992 Te Deum [for 3 choirs, prepared piano, string orchestra and phonogram]
- 1986/1990 Festina lente [for string orchestra and harp ad lib.]
- 1988/1991 Sieben Magnificat-Antiphonen [for mixed choir a cappella]
  - 2008 O-Antiphonen [for 8 violoncellos]
- 1989 Magnificat [for mixed choir a cappella]
- 1989 Mein Weg hat Gipfel und Wellentäler [for organ]
  - 1999/2000 Mein Weg [for 14 string and percussion]
- 1989/1992 Miserere [for soloists, mixed choir, instrumental ensemble and organ]
- 1989/1997 Nïnye k vam. Ode IX from "Kanon pokajanen" [for mixed choir a cappella]
- 1990/1991 The Beatitudes [for mixed choir or soloists SATB and organ]
  - 2001 Beatitudines [for mixed choir and organ]
- 1990 Bogoróditse Djévo. Mother of God and Virgin [for mixed choir a cappella]
- 1990 Statuit ei Dominus [for 2 mixed choirs and 2 organs]
  - 2011 Statuit ei Dominus [for 2 mixed choirs, 8 wind instruments and string orchestra]
- 1990/1996 Beatus Petronius [for 2 mixed choirs and 2 organs]
  - 2011 Beatus Petronius [for 2 mixed choirs, 8 wind instruments, bells and string orchestra]
- 1990/2002 Berliner Messe [for mixed choir or soloists SATB and organ]
  - 2002 Berliner Messe [for mixed choir and string orchestra]

- 2002 Credo from "Berliner Messe." Matzelsdorfer's version [for mixed choir or soloists SATB and organ]
- 2005 Credo from "Berliner Messe." Matzelsdorfer's version [for mixed choir and string orchestra]
- 1991 Silouan's Song. "My soul yearns after the Lord . . . " [for string orchestra]
  - 2012 Silouan's Song. "My soul yearns after the Lord . . . " [for 8 violoncellos]
- 1992 And One of the Pharisees . . . St Luke 7, 36–50 [for 3 voices or three-part choir Ct(A)TB a cappella]
- 1992/2005 Mozart-Adagio [for violin, violoncello and piano]
- 1992/1994 Trisagion [for string orchestra]
- 1994/1996 Litany. Prayers of St John Chrysostom for each hour of the day and night [for soloists A(Ct)TTB, mixed choir and orchestra]
- 1994/1997 Memento. Ode VII from "Kanon pokajanen" [for mixed choir a cappella]
- 1995/1999 Darf ich . . . [for solo violin, bell ad lib. and string orchestra]
- 1996/1998 Dopo la vittoria. Piccola cantata [for mixed choir a cappella]
- 1996 I Am the True Vine. St John 15, 1–14 [for mixed choir a cappella]
- 1997 Kanon pokajanen [for mixed choir a cappella]
  - 1997 Ode I from "Kanon pokajanen" [for mixed choir a cappella]
  - 1997 Ode III from "Kanon pokajanen" [for mixed choir a cappella]
  - 1997 Ode IV from "Kanon pokajanen" [for mixed choir a cappella]

- 1997 Ode V from "Kanon pokajanen" [for mixed choir a
  cappella]
- 1997 Ode VI – Kontakion – Ikos from "Kanon pokajanen" [for
  mixed choir a cappella]
- 1997 Ode VIII from "Kanon pokajanen" [for mixed choir a
  cappella]
- 1997 Prayer after the Canon from "Kanon pokajanen" [for
  mixed choir a cappella]
- 1997 The Woman with the Alabaster Box. St Matthew 26, 6–13
  [for mixed choir a cappella]
- 1997 Tribute to Caesar. St Matthew 22, 15–22 [for mixed choir
  a cappella]
- 1998 Triodion [for mixed choir a cappella]
- 1998 Zwei Beter. St Luke 18, 9–14 [for female choir a cappella]
- 1998/2002 Como cierva sedienta. Psalm 42–43 (41–42) [for
  soprano or female choir and orchestra]
- 1999/2002 Cantique des degrés. Psalm 121 (120) [for mixed
  choir and orchestra]
- 2000 Orient & Occident [for string orchestra]
- 2000/2002 Cecilia, vergine romana [for mixed choir and
  orchestra]
- 2000 Littlemore Tractus [for mixed choir and organ]
  - 2013 Swan Song. Littlemore Tractus [for orchestra]
- 2000 My Heart's in the Highlands [for countertenor (or alto)
  and organ]
  - 2013 My Heart's in the Highlands [for countertenor (or alto),
    violin, viola, violoncello and piano]
- 2000 Which Was the Son of . . . St Luke 3, 23–38 [for mixed
  choira cappella]
- 2001 Nunc dimittis. St Luke 2, 29–32 [for mixed choir a
  cappella]

- 2001 Salve Regina [for mixed choir and organ]
- 2011 Salve Regina [for mixed choir, celesta and string orchestra]
- 2002 Peace upon you, Jerusalem. Psalm 122 (121) [for female choir a cappella]
- 2002 Estonian Lullaby / Eesti hällilaul. Kuss-kuss, kallike [for 2 female voices and piano]
  - 2006 Estonian Lullaby / Eesti hällilaul. Kuss-kuss, kallike [for female choir or 2 female voices and string orchestra]
  - 2009 Estonian Lullaby / Eesti hällilaul. Kuss-kuss, kallike [for female voice, 4 violas and 4 violoncellos]
- 2002 Christmas Lullaby / Rozhdyestvyenskaya kolïbyelnaya. St Luke 2, 7 [for female voice and piano]
  - 2006 Christmas Lullaby / Rozhdyestvyenskaya kolïbyelnaya. St Luke 2, 7 [for female choir or one female voice and string orchestra]
  - 2009 Christmas Lullaby / Rozhdyestvyenskaya kolïbyelnaya. St Luke 2, 7 [for female voice, 4 violas and 4 violoncellos]
- 2002 Lamentate. Homage to Anish Kapoor and his sculpture 'Marsyas' [for piano and orchestra]
- 2003 In principio. St John 1, 1–14 [for mixed choir and orchestra]
- 2003 Most Holy Mother of God [for 4 voices Ct(A)TTB a cappella]
- 2003 Passacaglia [for violin and piano]
  - 2007 Passacaglia [for 1 or 2 violins, vibraphone ad lib. and string orchestra]
- 2004 L'abbé Agathon [for soprano and 8 violoncellos]
  - 2005 L'abbé Agathon [for soprano, 4 violas and 4 violoncellos]
  - 2008 L'abbé Agathon [for 2 soloists SA(B), female choir and string orchestra]

- 2004 Anthem of St John the Baptist. St John 1, 29–34 [for mixed choir and organ]
- 2004 Da pacem Domine [four-part music, without fixed instrumentation]
  - 2006 Da pacem Domine [for mixed choir or soloists SATB a cappella]
  - 2006 Da pacem Domine [for mixed choir and string orchestra]
  - 2006 Da pacem Domine [for string quartet]
  - 2006 Da pacem Domine [for string orchestra]
  - 2007 Da pacem Domine [for recorder quartet]
  - 2008 Da pacem Domine [for mixed choir and orchestra]
  - 2009 Da pacem Domine [for saxophone quartet]
  - 2010 Da pacem Domine [for 8 or 4 violoncellos]
- 2005 Von Angesicht zu Angesicht. 1st Corinthians 13, 12 [for soprano, baritone, clarinet, viola and contrabass]
- 2005 La Sindone [for orchestra]
- 2005/2011 Vater unser [for boy-soprano or countertenor (or children's choir unisono) and piano]
  - 2013 Vater unser [for boy-soprano or countertenor and string orchestra or string quartet]
- 2006 Estländler [for flute]
  - 2009 Estländler [for violin]
- 2006 Für Anna Maria [for piano]
- 2006 Für Lennart in memoriam [for string orchestra]
- 2006 Veni creator [for mixed choir or soloists SATB and organ]
  - 2010 Veni creator [for mixed choir and string orchestra]
- 2007 The Deer's Cry [for mixed choir a cappella]
- 2007 Morning Star [for mixed choir a cappella]
- 2007 Scala cromatica. Trio piccolo [for violin, violoncello and piano]

- 2007 Sei gelobt, du Baum [for baritone, violin, quinterne (or mandolin or lute) and contrabass]
- 2008 Alleluia-Tropus [for vocal ensemble or chamber choir SATB and 8 violoncellos ad lib.]
  - 2010 Alleluia-Tropus [for mixed choir and string orchestra]
- 2008 "These words . . . " [for string orchestra and percussion]
- 2008 Symphony No. 4 "Los Angeles" [for string orchestra, harp, timpani and percussion]
- 2009/2010 Silhouette. Hommage à Gustave Eiffel [for large string orchestra and percussion]
- 2009 Missa brevis [for 12 violoncellos]
  - 2010 Missa brevis [for 8 violoncellos]
- 2010 Adam's Lament [for mixed choir and string orchestra]
- 2012 Habitare fratres in unum. Psalm 133 (132) [for mixed choir SA(Ct)TB or vocal ensemble S(Ct)A(Ct)TB a cappella]
- 2012/2013 Virgencita [for mixed choir a cappella]
- 2014 Drei Hirtenkinder aus Fátima [for mixed choir a cappella]

II. Selected Further Reading on the Orthodox Church

Apart from the texts on specific subjects or persons that I refer to in this book, the following are a few general introductions to the theology, history, and structure of the Orthodox Church, listed in alphabetical order.

Peter C. Bouteneff, *Sweeter Than Honey: Orthodox Thinking on Dogma and Truth* (Crestwood, NY: St Vladimir's Seminary Press, 2006).

Olivier Clément, *The Roots of Christian Mysticism* (London: New City, 1993).

Andrew Louth, *Introducing Eastern Orthodox Theology* (Downers Grove, IL: InterVarsity, 2013).

John Anthony McGuckin, *The Orthodox Church: An Introduction to Its History, Doctrine, and Spiritual Culture* (Oxford: Blackwell, 2008).

Timothy (Kallistos) Ware, *The Orthodox Church* (Penguin, 1993).

Timothy (Kallistos) Ware, *The Orthodox Way* (Crestwood, NY: St Vladimir's Seminary Press, 1999).

III. Adam's Lament[2]

Arvo Pärt's 2010 composition "Adam's Lament" sets the first portion of St Silouan's meditation, about 1/5 of it. The text is reproduced below in its entirety to allow for a deeper immersion into its spirit, and to shed greater light on its author.

Adam, father of all mankind, in paradise knew the sweetness of the love of God; and so when for his sin he was driven forth from the Garden of Eden, and was widowed of the love of God, he suffered grievously and lamented with a mighty moan. And the whole desert rang with his lamentations, for his soul was racked as he thought, "I have grieved my beloved Lord." He sorrowed less after paradise and the beauty thereof—he sorrowed that he was bereft of the love of God, which insatiably, at every instant, draws the soul to Him.

In the same way the soul which has known God through the Holy Spirit, but has afterwards lost grace experiences the torment that Adam suffered. There is an aching and a deep regret in the soul that has grieved the beloved Lord.

Adam pined on earth, and wept bitterly, and the earth was not pleasing to him. He was heartsick for God, and this was his cry:

"My soul wearies for the Lord, and I seek Him in tears.
"How should I not seek Him?
"When I was with Him my soul was glad and at rest,
and the enemy could not come nigh me.
"But now the spirit of evil has gained power over me,

---

[2]Reproduced from *Saint Silouan the Athonite* (Crestwood, NY: St Vladimir's Seminary Press, 1999), 448–456, with gratitude to the Patriarchal Stavropegic Monastery of St. John the Baptist for their kind blessing.

harassing and oppressing my soul,
"so that I weary for the Lord even unto death,
"and my spirit strains to God,
and there is nought on earth can make me glad,
"Nor can my soul take comfort in any thing,
but longs once more to see the Lord,
that her hunger may be appeased.

"I cannot forget Him for a single moment,
and my soul languishes after Him,
"and from the multitude of my afflictions
I lift up my voice and cry:
" 'Have mercy upon me, O God. Have mercy on Thy fallen
 creature.' "

Thus did Adam lament,
and the tears steamed down his face on to his beard,
on to the ground beneath his feet,
and the whole desert heard the sound of his moaning.
The beasts and the birds were hushed in grief;
while Adam wept because peace and love were lost to all
men on account of his sin.

Adam knew great grief when he was banished from paradise,
but when he saw his son Abel slain by Cain his brother, Adam's
 grief was even heavier.
His soul was heavy, and he lamented and thought:

"Peoples and nations will descend from me, and multiply, and
 suffering will be their
lot, and they will live in enmity and seek to slay one another."

And his sorrow stretched wide as the sea, and only the soul that
   has come to
know the Lord and the magnitude of His love for us can
   understand.

I, too, have lost grace and call with Adam:
"Be merciful unto me, O Lord! Bestow on me the spirit of humility
   and love."[3]

O love of the Lord! He who has known Thee seeks Thee, tireless,
   day and night, crying with a loud voice:

"I pine for Thee, O Lord, and seek Thee in tears.
"How should I not seek Thee?
'Thou didst give me to know Thee by the Holy Spirit,
"And in her knowing of God my soul is drawn to seek Thee in
   tears."

Adam wept:
"The desert cannot pleasure me;
nor the high mountains, nor meadow nor forest,
nor the singing of birds.
"I have no pleasure in any thing.
"My soul sorrows with a great sorrow:
"I have grieved God.
"And were the Lord to set me down in paradise again,
"There, too, would I sorrow and weep–
'O why did I grieve my beloved God?' "

The soul of Adam fell sick when he was exiled from paradise,
and many were the tears he shed in his distress.

---

[3]Here ends the portion of the text that is sung in Pärt's *Adam's Lament*.

Likewise every soul that has known the Lord yearns for Him, and
    cries:

"Where art Thou, O Lord? Where art Thou, my Light?
"Why hast Thou hidden Thy face from me?
"Long is it since my soul beheld Thee,
"And she wearies after Thee and seeks Thee in tears.
"Where is my Lord?
"Why is it that my soul sees Him not?
"What hinders Him from dwelling in me?"

This hinders Him: Christ-like humility and love for my enemies art
    not in me.

God is love insaturable, love impossible to describe.

Adam walked the earth, weeping from his heart's manifold ills,
    while the thoughts of his mind were on God;
And when his body grew faint, and he could no longer shed tears,
    still his spirit burned with longing for God,
For he could not forget paradise and the beauty thereof.
But even more was it the power of His love which caused the soul
    of Adam to reach out towards God.

I write of thee, O Adam;
But thou art witness, my feeble understanding cannot fathom thy
    longing after God,
Nor how thou didst carry the burden of repentance.
O Adam, thou dost see how I, thy child, suffer here on earth.
Small is the fire within me,
and the flame of my love flickers low.
O Adam, sing unto us the song of the Lord,
That my soul may rejoice in the Lord

And be moved to praise and glorify Him
as the Cherubim and Seraphim praise Him in the heavens,
And all the hosts of heavenly angels sing to Him the thrice-holy
    hymn.
O Adam, our father, sing unto us the Lord's song,
That the whole earth may hear,
and all thy sons may lift their minds to God
and delight in the strains of the heavenly anthem,
And forget their sorrows on earth.

The Holy Spirit is love and sweetness for the soul, mind and body.
And those who have come to know God by the Holy Spirit stretch
upward day and night, insatiable, to the living God, for the love
of God is exceeding sweet. But when the soul loses grace, her tears
flow as she seeks the Holy Spirit anew.

But the man who has not known God through the Holy Spirit
cannot seek Him with tears, and his soul is ever harrowed by the
passions; his mind is on earthly things. Contemplation is not for
him, and he cannot come to know Jesus Christ. Jesus Christ is
made known through the Holy Spirit.

Adam knew God in paradise, and after his fall sought Him in tears.

O Adam, our father, tell us, thy sons, of the Lord.
Thy soul didst know God on earth,
Knew paradise too, and the sweetness and gladness thereof,
And now thou livest in heaven
and dost behold the glory of the Lord.
Tell of how our Lord is glorified for His sufferings.
Speak to us of the songs that are sung in heaven,
how sweet they are, for they are sung in the Holy Spirit.

Tell us of the glory of the Lord,
of His great mercy and how He loveth His creature.
Tell us of the Most Holy Mother of God,
how she is magnified in the heavens,
And the hymns that call her blessed.
Tell us how the Saints rejoice there, radiant with grace.
Tell us how they love the Lord,
and in what humility they stand before God.

O Adam, comfort and cheer our troubled souls.
Speak to us of the things thou dost behold in heaven . . .

Why art thou silent? . . . Lo, the whole earth is in travail . . .
Art thou so filled with the love of God that thou canst not think of
      us?
Or thou beholdest the Mother of God in glory,
and canst not tear thyself from the sight,
and wouldst not bestow a word of tenderness on us who sorrow,
that we might forget the affliction there is on earth?
O Adam, our father, thou dost see the wretchedness of thy sons on
      earth.
Why then art thou silent?

And Adam speaks:
"My children, leave me in peace.
"I cannot wrench myself from the love of God to speak with you.
"My soul is wounded with love of the Lord, and rejoices in His
      beauty.
"How should I remember the earth?
"Those who live before the Face of the Most High cannot think on
      earthly things."

O Adam, our father, thou hast forsaken us, thine orphans,
though misery is our portion here on earth.
Tell us what we may do to be pleasing to God?
Look upon thy children scattered over the face of the earth,
our minds scattered, too.
Many have forgotten God.
They live in darkness and journey to the abyss of hell.

"Trouble me not. I see the Mother of God in glory—
"How can I tear myself away to speak with you?
"I see the holy Prophets and Apostles;
and they are in the likeness of our Lord Jesus Christ, Son of God.
"I walk in the gardens of paradise,
and everywhere behold the glory of the Lord.
"For the Lord is in me and hath made me like unto Himself."

O Adam yet we are thy children!
Tell us in our tribulation how we may inherit paradise,
that we, like thee, may behold the glory of the Lord.
Our souls long for the Lord, while thou dost live in heaven
and rejoice in the glory of the Lord.

"Why cry ye out to me, my children?
"The Lord loveth you and hath given you commandments.
"Be faithful to them, love one another,
and ye shall find rest in God.
"Let not an hour pass without ye repent of your transgressions,
that ye may be ready to meet the Lord.
"The Lord said: 'I love them that love me,
and glorify them that glorify me.'"

O Adam, pray for us, thy children.
Our souls are sad from many sorrows.

O Adam, our father, thou dwellest in heaven
and dost behold the Lord seated in glory
on the right hand of God the Father.
Thou dost see the Cherubim and Seraphim and all the Saints,
and dost hear celestial songs,
whose sweetness maketh thy soul forgetful of the earth.
But we here on earth are sad, and we weary greatly after God.
There is little fire within us
with which ardently to love the Lord.
Inspire us, what must we do to gain paradise?

Adam makes answer:

"Leave me in peace, my children,
for from sweetness of the love of God
I cannot think about the earth."

O Adam, our souls are weary,
and we are heavy-laden with sorrow.
Speak a word of comfort to us.
Sing to us from the songs thou hearest in heaven,
that the whole earth may hear and men forget their afflictions . . .
O Adam, we are very sad.

"Leave me in peace. The time of my tribulation is past.
"From the beauty of paradise and the sweetness of the Holy Spirit I
      can no longer be mindful of the earth.
"But this I tell you:
"The Lord loveth you, and do you live in love and be obedient to
      those in authority over you.
"Humble your hearts, and the Spirit of God will live in you.
"He cometh softly into the soul and giveth her peace,
and beareth wordless witness to salvation.

"Sing to God in love and lowliness of Spirit,
for the Lord rejoiceth therein."

O Adam, our father, what are we to do?
We sing, but love and humility are not in us.

"Repent before the Lord, and entreat of Him.
"He loveth man and will give all things.
"I, too, repented deeply and sorrowed much that I had grieved
     God,
"And that peace and love were lost on earth because of my sin.
"My tears ran down my face. My breast was wet with my tears,
and the earth under my feet;
and the desert heard the sound of my moaning.
"You cannot apprehend my sorrow,
nor how I lamented after God and paradise.
"In paradise was I joyful and glad:
the Spirit of God rejoiced me,
and suffering was a stranger to me.
"But when I was driven forth from paradise
cold and hunger began to torment me.
"The beasts and the birds that were gentle and had loved
me turned into wild things
and were afraid and ran from me.
"Evil thoughts goaded me.
"The sun and the wind scorched me.
"The rain fell on me.
"I was plagued by sickness and all the afflictions of the earth.
"But I endured all things, trusting steadfastly in God.

"Do ye, then, bear the travail of repentance.
"Greet tribulation. Wear down your bodies. Humble yourselves

and love your enemies,
that the Holy Spirit may take up His abode in you,
and then shall ye know and attain the Kingdom of Heaven.

"But come not nigh me:
"Now from love of God have I forgotten the earth
and all that therein is.
"Forgotten even is the paradise I lost,
for I behold the glory of the Lord,
and the glory of the Saints whom the light of God's countenance
maketh radiant as the Lord Himself."

O Adam, sing unto us a heavenly song,
that the whole earth may hearken,
and delight in the peace of love towards God.
We would hear those songs.
Sweet are they for they are sung in the Holy Spirit.

Adam lost the earthly paradise and sought it weeping. But the Lord through His love on the Cross gave Adam another paradise, fairer than the old—a paradise in heaven where shines the Light of the Holy Trinity.

What shall we render unto the Lord for His love to us?

IV. The Arvo Pärt Project at St Vladimir's Seminary

This book grew out of the Arvo Pärt Project, an endeavor to celebrate and study the composer's work in light of his relationship to the Orthodox Church. The Project occasioned Pärt's first visit to New York in thirty years, as well as the conferral of an honorary doctorate by St Vladimir's Orthodox Theological Seminary. This was the first of Pärt's eleven honorary doctorates to date that was given by an Orthodox Christian institution.

A. Conferral by St Vladimir's Seminary of the Degree of Doctor of Music, *honoris causa*, May 31, 2014. Citation.

Maestro Arvo Pärt

A world-renowned composer—the most-performed living composer in the world today—you have given your life to the creation of a vast body of musical compositions that have been received by a diverse and devoted listenership. Your fervent admirers, regardless of their religious faith, perceive in your work the breath of the Spirit.

Your music reaches people where they are—as seekers of God,
  seekers of truth, seekers of purity—and nourishes their way;
Your works bring the Holy Scriptures—notably the Psalms, the
  Passion of Our Lord, the prologue of the Holy Evangelist
  John—into a new light, revealing in them new depths;
Your settings of sacred texts and prayers highlight their purity and
  profundity. Through these compositions, you invite the world

on a journey towards the love of God and the repentance of
  sins—a journey from the Old Adam to the New Adam;

Your musical work, both with and without text, weaves the
  inextricable threads of suffering and of consolation, of loss
  and of hope, of sin and forgiveness, in ways that are accessible
  to people from all walks of life, especially to those who are
  themselves suffering;

An Orthodox Christian steeped in the Church, through its Fathers
  and its liturgical and prayer life, your oeuvre breathes its ethos,
  even as it testifies to your broadly ecumenical heart;

A spiritual son of Archimandrite Sophrony, you have given musical
  life to his teachings, most especially through your settings of
  the texts of his own *staretz*, St Silouan of Mount Athos;

In all, you have become a true minister of the Word, inspiring,
  consoling, challenging, and enlightening all those who hear
  your music.

In recognition of your immeasurable contribution, which, conso-
nant with the mission of St Vladimir's Seminary, represents a deep
penetration of contemporary culture by the life and teaching of
the Church, we are pleased to affirm that:

By virtue of the power vested in the Board of Trustees and the
Faculty of St Vladimir's Orthodox Theological Seminary by the
Board of Regents of the University of the State of New York, the
degree of Doctor of Sacred Music *honoris causa* is bestowed upon
Arvo Pärt.

B. Arvo Pärt, Commencement Address
St Vladimir's Orthodox Theological Seminary, May 31, 2014[4]

Your Beatitude, Your Graces, Your Honor the Minister of Culture, and Your Excellency the Ambassador, Reverend Fathers, and friends in Christ!

It is fitting at such a dignified ceremony to express some words of thanks.

Please allow me to express these with some thoughts from my musical diaries. These are my daily workbooks in which, over the decades, I have recorded my reflections both in musical notation and in words.

* * *

In the Pühtitsa monastery:

"Have you thanked God for this failure already?" These unexpected words were said by a little girl.

I remember exactly: it was July 25, 1976. I was sitting in the monastery yard, on a bench in the shadow of the bushes, with my notebook.

"What are you writing there?" the girl, who was around ten, asked me.

"I am trying to write music, but it's not turning out well," I said.

And then the unexpected words from her: "Have you thanked God for this failure already?"

[4]Translated from the Estonian by Marrit Andrejeva, with minor emendations after delivery.

Like me, that little priest's daughter from Russia was a visitor to the monastery, with her father.

* * *

The most sensitive musical instrument is the human soul. The next is the human voice.

One must purify the soul until it begins to sound.

A composer is a musical instrument and at the same time, a performer on that instrument.

The instrument has to be in order to produce sound. One must start with that, not with the music. Through the music, the composer can check whether his instrument is tuned, and to what key it is tuned.

* * *

God knits man in his mother's womb slowly and wisely. Art should be born in a similar way.

* * *

To be like a beggar when it comes to writing music—whatever, however, and whenever God gives.

We shouldn't grieve because of writing little and poorly, but because we pray little and poorly and lukewarmly, and live in the wrong way.

* * *

The criterion must be *everywhere and only* humility.

Palestrina's melodies should be viewed (assessed) in this way too.

This is where lies their mysterious "nobility."

* * *

Music is my friend: ever-understanding, compassionate, forgiving. It's a comforter, the handkerchief for drying my tears of sadness, the source of my tears of joy, my liberation and flight. But also a painful thorn in my flesh and soul, that which makes me sober and teaches humility.

BIBLIOGRAPHY

Athanasius of Alexandria. "Letter to Marcellinus." In *Athanasius: The Life of Antony and the Letter to Marcellinus*, edited by Robert C. Gregg. New York: Paulist, 1980.

Batuman, Elif. "The Bells: How Harvard Helped Preserve a Russian Legacy." *The New Yorker*, April 27, 2009.

Beauchamp, Paul. *Création et séparation: Étude exégétique du chapitre premier de la Genèse*. Lectio Divina. Paris: Cerf, 2005 [1969].

Begbie, Jeremy S. *Resounding Truth: Christian Wisdom in the World of Music*. Engaging Culture. Grand Rapids, MI: Baker Academic, 2007.

Bostonia, Marguerite. "Bells as Inspiration for Tintinnabulation." In *The Cambridge Companion to Arvo Pärt*, edited by Andrew Shenton, 128–139. Cambridge: Cambridge University Press, 2012.

Bouteneff, Peter C. *Beginnings: Ancient Christian Readings of the Biblical Creation Narratives*. Grand Rapids, MI: Baker Academic, 2008.

———. "Christ and Salvation." In *The Cambridge Companion to Orthodox Christian Theology*, edited by Mary B. Cunningham and Elizabeth Theokritoff, 93–106. Cambridge: Cambridge University Press, 2008.

———. Recorded Interview with Arvo and Nora Pärt. Laulasmaa, Estonia: unpublished, March 14, 2014.

————. *Sweeter Than Honey: Orthodox Thinking on Dogma and Truth*. Foundations Series. Crestwood, NY: St Vladimir's Seminary Press, 2006.

Brauneiss, Leopold. "Musical Archetypes: The Basic Elements of the Tintinnabuli Style." In *The Cambridge Companion to Arvo Pärt* edited by Andrew Shenton, 49–75. Cambridge: Cambridge University Press, 2012.

————. "Tintinnabuli: An Introduction." Translated by Robert Crow. In *Arvo Pärt in Conversation*, edited by Enzo Restagno, et al., 109–62. Champagne, IL: Dalkey Archive, 2012.

————. "The Unification of Opposites: The Tintinnabuli Style in the Light of the Philosophy of Nicolaus Cusanus." *Music and Literature* 1, no. 1 (2012): 53–60.

Brueggemann, Walter. "The Formfulness of Grief." *Interpretation* 31 (1977): 263–75.

————. "From Hurt to Joy, from Death to Life." *Interpretation* 28 (1974): 3–19.

Carrette, Jeremy, and Richard King. *Selling Spirituality: The Silent Takeover of Religion*. Abingdon, UK: Routledge, 2005.

Clarke, David. "Parting Glances: Aesthetic Solace or Act of Complicity?" *Musical Times* 134, no. 1810 (1993): 680–84.

Cubitt, Sean. *The Practice of Light: A Genealogy of Visual Technologies from Prints to Pixels*. The Leonardo Series. Cambridge, MA: Massachusetts Institute of Technology, 2014.

Davis, Ellen F. "Exploding the Limits: Form and Function in Psalm 22." *Journal for the Study of the Old Testament* 53 (1992): 93–105.

Demacopoulos, George, and Aristotle Papanikolaou, eds. *Orthodox Constructions of the West*. Orthodox Christianity and Contemporary Thought. New York: Fordham University Press, 2013.

Dolp, Laura. "Arvo Pärt in the Marketplace." In *The Cambridge Companion to Arvo Pärt*, edited by Andrew Shenton, 177–92. Cambridge: Cambridge University Press, 2012.

Douglas, Mary. *Purity and Danger: An Analysis of Concepts of Pollution and Taboo*. London: Routledge, 1966.

Drozzina, Sasha. "The Music of Arvo Pärt at Koerner Hall." http:// bachtrack.com/review-toronto-arvo-part.

Durkheim, Emil. *The Elementary Forms of Religious Life*. Translated by Carol Edelman. Oxford: Oxford University Press, 2001 [1912].

Eliade, Mircea. *The Sacred and the Profane: The Nature of Religion*. Translated by Willard R. Trask. New York: Harcourt Brace, 1959.

Elste, Martin. "An Interview with Arvo Pärt." *Fanfare* 11, no. March/ April (1988): 337–41.

Fisk, Josiah. "The New Simplicity: The Music of Górecki, Tavener, and Pärt." *The Hudson Review* 47, no. 3 (1994): 394–412.

Harmless, William. *Desert Chrstians: An Introduction to the Literature of Early Monasticism*. Oxford: Oxford University Press, 2004.

Hart, David Bentley. *The Beauty of the Infinite: The Aesthetics of Christian Truth*. Grand Rapids, MI: Eerdmans, 2003.

Hillier, Paul. *Arvo Pärt*. Oxford Studies of Composers. Oxford: Oxford University Press, 1997.

Hopko, Thomas. "The Trinity in the Cappadocians." In *Christian Spirituality: Origins to the Twelfth Century*, edited by Bernard McGinn and John Meyendorff, 260–75. New York: Crossroad, 1987.

Johnson, Christopher D.L. *The Globalization of Hesychasm and the Jesus Prayer: Contesting Contemplation*. Continuum Advances in Religion. New York and London: Continuum, 2010.

———. " 'He Has Made the Dry Bones Live': Orientalism's Attempted Resuscitation of Eastern Christianity." *Journal of the American Academy of Religion* 82, no. 3 (2014): 811–40.

Kelman, John. "Manfred Eicher: Through the Lens." In *All About Jazz*, October 31, 2011.

Kõrver, Kristina, Kai Kutman, Hedi Rosma, eds. *In Principio: The Word in Arvo Pärt's Music*. Laulasmaa, Estonia: Arvo Pärt Centre, 2014.

Lewis, C.S. *The Screwtape Letters*. San Francisco, CA: Harper Collins, 2001 [1941].

Lingas, Alexander. "From Earth to Heaven: The Changing Soundscape of Byzantine Liturgy." In *Experiencing Byzantium: Papers from the 44th Spring Symposium of Byzantine Studies, Newcastle and Durham, April 2011*, edited by Claire Nesbitt and Mark Jackson. Society for the Promotion of Byzantine Studies Publications, 311–58. Aldershot: Ashgate, 2013.

————. "Preliminary Reflections on Studying the Liturgical Place of Byzantine and Slavonic Melismatic Chant." In *Paleobyzantine Notations III: Acta of the Congress Held at Hernen Castle, the Netherlands, in March 2001*, edited by Gerda Wolfram. Eastern Christian Studies, 147–55. Leuven, Paris, and Dudley, MA: Peeters, 2004.

Lubow, Arthur. "Arvo Pärt: The Sound of Spirit." *The New York Times Magazine*, October 15, 2010.

Luibheid, Colm, and Norman Russell, eds., trans. *John Climacus: The Ladder of Divine Ascent*. Classics of Western Spirituality. New Jersey: Paulist, 1982.

Luptakova, Marina. "The Nature and Origin of Evil According to the Eastern Christian Church." In *The Ethics of Terrorism: Innovative Approaches from an International Perspective*, edited by Yakov Gilinskiy, Thomas Albert Gilly, Vladimir A. Sergevnin, 218–23. Springfield, IL: Charles Thomas, 2009.

MacMillan, James. "Divine Accompaniment." *The Guardian*, July 18, 2003.

Maimets-Volt, Kaire. "Mediating the 'Idea of One': Arvo Pärt's Pre-Existing Film Music." Estonian Academy of Music and Theatre, 2009.

Mattner, Lothar. "Arvo Pärt: *Tabula Rasa*." *Music and Literature* 1, no. 1 (2012): 29–52.

McKinnon, James, ed. *Music in Early Christian Literature*. Cambridge, UK: Cambridge University Press, 1987.

Mellers, Wilfrid. "Arvo Pärt, God and Gospel: *Passio Domini Nostri Iesu Christi Secundum Iohannem* [Sic]." *Contemporary Music Review* 12, no. 2 (1995): 35–48.

————. *Celestial Music? Some Masterpieces of European Religious Music*. Woodbridge, UK: Boydell, 2002.

Merton, Thomas. "Philosophy of Solitude." In *Disputed Questions*. New York: Farrar, Straus, & Cudahy, 1960.

Moody, Ivan. *Modernism and Orthodox Spirituality in Contemporary Music*. Joensuu, Finland: International Society for Orthodox Church Music, 2014.

Moody, Rick. *On Celestial Music, and Other Adventures in Listening*. New York: Little, Brown & Co., 2012.

Müller, Lars. *ECM: Sleeves of Desire: A Cover Story*. Princeton: Princeton Architectural Press, 1996.

————. *Windfall Light: The Visual Language of ECM*. Zürich: Lars Müller Publishers, 2010.

Nestor, Siim. "Arvo Pärt: 'Ju me siis salaja . . .'." *Eesti Ekspress*, September 11, 2010.

The New Grove Dictionary of Music and Musicians. 20 vols. London: Macmillan, 1980.

Ng, David. "When Classical Music Masterpieces Become Soundtrack Clichés." In *Culture Monster*. Los Angeles: *Los Angeles Times*, 2008.

Nouwen, Henri. *The Way of the Heart: Desert Spirituality and Contemporary Ministry*. San Francisco, CA: Harper & Row, 1981.

Restagno, Enzo, Leopold Brauneiss, Saale Kareda, Arvo Pärt. *Arvo Pärt in Conversation*. Translated by Robert Crow. Champaign, IL: Dalkey Archive, 2012. Translation of *Arvo Pärt im Gespräch*. Vienna: Universal Editions AG, 2010.

Ricoeur, Paul. *On Translation*. Translated by Eileen Brennan. London & New York: Routledge, 2006.

Ricoeur, Paul, and André LaCocque. *Thinking Biblically: Exegetical and Hermeneutical Studies*. Chicago: University of Chicago, 2003.

Robin, William. "His Music, Entwined with His Faith." *The New York Times*, May 16, 2014.

Ross, Alex. "Consolations: The Uncanny Voice of Arvo Pärt." *The New Yorker*, December 2, 2002.

Sakharov, Archimandrite Sophrony. *Saint Silouan the Athonite*. Translated by Rosemary Edmonds. Crestwood, NY: St Vladimir's Seminary Press, 1999 [1991].

Sakharov, Nicholas V. *I Love Therefore I Am: The Theological Legacy of Archimandrite Sophrony*. Crestwood, NY: St Vladimir's Seminary Press, 2002.

Saler, Robert C. *Between Magisterium and Marketplace: A Constructive Account of Theology and the Church*. Emerging Scholars. Minneapolis, MN: Fortress, 2014.

Savall, Jordi. "A Conversation with Arvo Pärt." *Music and Literature* 1, no. 1 (2012): 7–14.

Schmemann, Alexander. *Great Lent: Journey to Pascha*, rev. edn. Crestwood, NY: St Vladimir's Seminary Press, 1974.

————. *Introduction to Liturgical Theology*. Crestwood, NY: St Vladimir's Seminary Press, 1975.

Schoenberg, Arnold. "The Relationship to the Text." In *Style and Idea: Selected Writings of Arnold Schoenberg*, edited by Leonard Stein, 141–45. Berkeley, CA: University of California Press, 1984 [1912].

Shenton, Andrew, ed. *The Cambridge Companion to Arvo Pärt*. Cambridge: Cambridge University Press, 2012.

Sholl, Robert. "Arvo Pärt and Spirituality." In *The Cambridge Companion to Arvo Pärt* edited by Andrew Shenton, 140–58. Cambridge: Cambridge University Press, 2012.

Sloane, Robert. "Tensions between Popular and Alternative Music: R.E.M. as an Artist-Intellectual." In *A Companion to Media Studies*, edited by Angharad N. Valdivia, 72–92. Oxford: Blackwell, 2003.

Smith, Geoff. "Sources of Invention: An Interview with Arvo Pärt." *The Musical Times* 140, no. 1868 (Autumn 1999): 19–25.

Supin, Dorian. *24 Preludes for a Fugue*. Documentary Film. 87 Min., 2002.

Taves, Ann. *Religious Experience Reconsidered: A Building-Block Approach to the Study of Religion and Other Special Things*. Princeton, NJ: Princeton University Press, 2009.

Taylor, Charles. *A Secular Age*. Cambridge, MA: Belknap/Harvard University Press, 2007.

Ward, Benedicta. *The Sayings of the Desert Fathers: The Alphabetical Collection*. London: Mowbray, 1975.

Wigley, Samuel. "Is It Time to Give Pärt a Rest?" In *Film Blog. The Guardian*, 2008.

Wortley, John, trans. *Give Me a Word: The Alphabetical Sayings of the Desert Fathers*. Popular Patristics Series 52. Yonkers, NY: St Vladimir's Seminary Press, 2014.

Zacharias, Archimandrite. *The Enlargement of the Heart : "Be Ye Also Enlarged" (2 Corinthians 6:13) in the Theology of Saint Silouan the Athonite and Elder Sophrony of Essex*. South Canaan, PA: Mount Thabor Publishing, 2006.